SOBER AS FUCK

SOBER
AS
FUCK

HOW I STARTED RECOVERY
AND TOOK AN INDUSTRY OUT
TO SAVE THE ADDICTED ME.

BY MANN ROBINSON

CONTENTS

SECTION IV: SOLVING A PROBLEM

THE ALCOHOL INDUSTRY

The money side of alcohol is the most fucked up part about it. The money that is spent on advertisements and endorsements creates the power to brainwash the world into thinking that getting drunk is shit and cool. Yet, you are the pawn in an industry that crosses the lines of corporations, governments, and private citizens. The alcohol industry is big business and is definitely recession-proof. Even the pandemic, COVID-19, couldn't affect the high profits earned from crazy mark-ups.

According to Statista.com, alcohol sales have spiked from $3.7 billion in 2017 to $6.4 billion in the 3rd quarter of 2020.

By the time the liquor gets in your hand, you have paid many people. Now, it's true that every item that you purchase in this world is sold for profit. But the difference with alcohol is that it is fucking up your life, all while making liquor companies and the people that own them rich as fuck. Governments are amassing revenue from taxation and assessing crazy fees from violations related to alcohol consumption. And the private citizen supports all this.

These liquor companies have what you would call "a dream." They are not responsible for your personal choices, no matter the advertising they portray. They operate without responsibility for the lives they've fucked up from overconsumption.

Governments become the enforcer of a vicious cycle of advertising, hope, consolation, self-medi cation, overconsumption, and legal trouble. Rater than support wellness, they are beneficiaries and labeled others with criminality.

Most companies are named after the person that started the company. Hennessy, Anheuser Bush, Seagrams, and so on. Let's be clear; I am a huge fan of business and entrepreneurs, but I hate to see people who are not on the high profit and big business side of the world's economic structure continually fucking up their lives while these companies rake in billions, year after year.

Their profit and loss statements do not include how Mann Robinson spent over $100,000 on D.U.I.s, fees, breathalyzers, insurance, and other types of shit they come up with.

Judges and prosecutors are elected based on their tough stance on crime, including D.U.I.s and other alcohol-related offenses. And the private citizens healing each day are tossed aside and labeled as alcoholic criminals. This point alone should make you want to stop drinking.

Maybe once I explain in later chapters how, by drinking, you may fuck up the lives of the people that you love, along with yours, you will wake the fuck up!

Prevalence of Alcohol

First of all, my neighborhood was only 5 square blocks. There was a church on every other corner. True! That was a repeated option. We also had six liquor stores surrounding those five blocks. This was a Black neighborhood surrounded by White neighborhoods. Growing up in this world, you'll know a specific set of truths handed down to us from the beginning of our lives. I was no different from those in my neighborhood when you look at our environment. Church or liquor stores. That's the choice and reality we grew up in. But the trap was set long ago.

Before slavery ended, Black people were so focused on the word "Free" that we were not prepared for anything else. We were free to buy and sell and make money. We were no longer sold, but goods were sold to us. People with means noticed this and provided an outlet for us to spend our money.

Slowly but surely, we became consumers rather than producers. We were handicapped from the jump. We are programmed through the media we consume. Now, we take liquor and glorify it. We create a lifestyle from our pain.

We even become accustomed to particular liquor. Nine times out of ten when you can see a person going into a store to buy alcohol, you can tell, just by looking at him, what kind of beer he is going to buy. If he is Black, he drinks Olde English 800. If I see a White dude on the corner, he is most likely drinking something like Miller (Ironically, both brands are owned by the same company, The Miller Brewing Company, founded by Fredrick Miller).

It is a cultural thing, but it is also a trap. We must get out of all the traps. We must know what our purpose is on the planet. Living in a consistently altered state of mind cannot be our purpose. Economics, influenced by greedy people, is about accessing the money caught up in your consumerism.

Much of the world is intentional about penalizing you and getting money out of you. Your purpose is subverted to fight for your rights, reduce your penalties, and resist (or protest) injustice. This is instead of seeking, expanding, and reinforcing your purpose.

You'll end up with no legacy to pass on to the next generation. It would help if you explore all the vices, people, and habits that are in your life and eliminate the toxins.

Know your value, lock in your purpose, and refuse the toxicity of consumerism. This is how you leave a legacy. My legacy is not in my failures but in how I overcame them. I am the perfect person to provide the answer to alcoholism for those who will listen. You can only teach and learn by example. If you have so many people outside the box attempting to teach people inside the box, it will not work.

Another institution is not the answer. Church, the State, and Social Clubs have too much power to penalize, deceive, and misinform. The solution is to connect with the source of your purpose and passion.

This is a relationship you must find. Whether you term it as, "God" or "a higher power," see it through realizing yourself as an individual. When you were first born (as a newborn baby), you were nervous and scared. After being cleaned up, you were placed in an incubator. No one was in that incubator with you. With that, no one will be in your casket when you die. Our entry and exit are alone, so why do you need someone else to build a connection between you and God? Please wake up and make that connection without the need for a community to process it for you. Beware of dependence upon celebrated citizens to define and compare yourself with.

SECTION I

ABOUT ME

CHAPTER 1

BEING A SPECIMEN

I sat on the bricked porch at our single-family home in Michigan when the Big Three motor companies still resided there. I was the five-year-old son of a hardworking father and an attentive mother.

My father had just taught me how to make paper airplanes, and I was throwing them off the porch and watching them fly. My friend, Deangelo Bailey, who lived five houses down from me, was walking by and saw the plane gliding through the air like a real one. He asked me to show him how to make them.

I do not know how it happened, but somehow, after playing, we walked around the neighborhood selling paper airplanes for 5 cents each. I did not know it then, but that was the first successful venture of my life. I was an entrepreneur to my core.

My father encouraged paper routes and other ventures as I got older. He signed me up to be a delivery boy for the local newspaper, but I did not do the paper route right at first. I would deliver to the list of houses they gave me, but when it was time to collect money at the end of the week, I would also collect from houses that were not on the list. People would pay the weekly fee even though they had not subscribed.

My enterprising nature did not stop there. I was also aware of trends. One day, I was delivering a newspaper to an older woman, and she saw a coupon for a free Faygo pop and one slice of pizza from the neighborhood store, Mr. C's deli.

I remember being just as excited as she was about the coupon because everybody in the hood loved their pizza.

So, I went through my stack of papers and cut out the coupon from every document. After delivering the rest of the newspapers without the page with coupons and advertisements, I sold the coupons around the neighborhood for 50 cents.

I didn't let my parents know I did this because I would have gotten into trouble. We were raised to do the right thing. Plus, my parents had a heavy influence on my decisions and choices. In high school elective selection, my mother put me in band class. "You never know when you will need an instrument," she said, but I knew I did not need an instrument. I realized later in life that her suggested choice of electives was heavily influenced by the Motown era.

I chose co-op instead the following year. It was a world of entrepreneurship with multiple skill development centers and business options. One kid in the school restaurant co-op always had the dopest sandwiches he made every day before lunch. He had fat-ass corned-beef sandwiches with everything on them, and everybody wanted one. He was also popular as a basketball player, so he could have sold anything, to be honest. But after seeing how crazy everybody was going over his sandwiches and how much money he was making, I joined the school restaurant and copied his entire system.

Other Lessons of Intrigue

Where I grew up, other lessons of hood entrepreneurship were prevalent. I watched drug dealers flaunt clothes, cars, money, and popularity on the block. I never sold drugs, but I saw it all, and the lifestyle was desirable.

They counted money fast and had all the girls. Everybody wanted what they had, especially me! One day, I was at the park, and I saw one drug dealer pay another. He took the money and didn't unfold it or count it. He put it up to his ear and smiled.

The other guy was like, "You ain't gone to count it?" And he replied, "Ain't no need. I can eyeball money." He just knew that it was $1000. As impressive as all of that was, the fear of spending time in prison became a reality after a few short summers. The short life came to an end. The powers then we're not about to let young black men make that type of money under the radar for long.

So, due to the strict drug laws, nationwide drug raids exploded in all significant inner cities. Sixty-eight young black men from my neighborhood were arrested in one night; my financial idols ended up with prison sentences ranging from 12 to 35 years.

It became a ghost town, with sadness and shock consuming the once highly active neighborhood. My father used this moment to press the importance of keeping it straight and narrow and working a legal nine to five. I still appreciate my parents for installing values into me, but the buy-low sell-high mentality that I picked up from the dope boys stuck with me forever.

In junior high, two different hustles were going on in the school. One was Jolly Ranchers candies. I don't know who brought them into school, but they were loaded with inventory and were selling like crazy. My favorite was fire (cinnamon), but this was short-lived as well. The principal caught wind of it and called the police to shut it down. The other hustle was Nerf footballs, monogrammed with college teams. In this case, somebody left a fully-stocked semi-truck parked near the neighborhood open. Hundreds, maybe thousands, of footballs made their way to our school and found themselves for sale.

For me, money-making was intriguing. I do not think it had anything to do with my household. We were still poor by government standards, but we never went hungry. I would watch my father get up and go to work every day. I didn't see it as getting more. I just thought it was intriguing. Along with their money-making, those salesmen/ dope boys were popular.

I learned later in life that when you run your own business, you are your business. Your success depends on how popular you are. It did not matter what the products were: sandwiches, drugs, or footballs. You must be likable.

Beyond likable and the level I understood as a child, an entrepreneur must be a leader—above the fray of consumerism and in control of the levers of supply, demand, and distribution. I was able to put it into words later in life. I knew I had to be a specimen. I had to be a man controlling his domain with vision and intention.

My first success began in failure. As an adult, I had regular jobs. One of my first was a temporary service job, making $18,000 a year. I hated working there. Yet I would work three to four times faster than the other workers around me. This was my period of paying my dues.

I learned to put my effort into whatever I did. I did not like the job, nor did I take pride in the work. I just felt like the faster I moved up, the quicker I could get out of there.

My method worked, and I was rising in the ranks. I was proud of the advancement, but as I said, I was not too fond of the experience. The level of pay did not help matters. I learned that I could do what needed to be done to make money. I also knew that you do not have to do only one thing. Your job is to expand your horizons and increase your options. That way, you can find what works for your bank account and happiness.

My supervisor, before I was promoted, was a woman of a certain age and attracted to me. I did not like her. I believe she was attracted to my work ethic, but she was also jealous. She was always over the top when dealing with me. It got to the point that I was filled with pure rage even hearing her voice.

One of my drivers was late returning from his route, and I took my frustration with her out on him. We got into an argument right after she had finished embarrassing me again. She came to me and went the extra mile to disrespect me for snapping at him. At that moment, I snapped at her, and she had no idea what was in me—the things that I'd seen growing up or the built-up hatred that I had for her.

With the situation so charged and my obvious hostile workplace complaint potential, I attended my exit interview half expecting that I would be vindicated and rehired. That is not the topic of discussion. I felt set up. It was the last disrespect I experienced there. If I never took what I now realize was a leap of faith to quit, I would not have made it to where I am today.

Rise of the Specimen

Two of my boys and I played little league football together. We were always together. One of them was the kid who got me my second newspaper delivery job. We set out to get people to sign up for the Detroit Free Press. We had to go house to house with a made-up story about raising money for our college fund. It was fun, but I was shy then and could not sell shit.

My boys were getting every other person to sign up, and they rubbed in my face daily. The point is, I knew that my boy was a solid salesman. I knew he was a natural. He worked at Circuit City, made $56k per year, and offered to put in a good word for me—the out-of-work factory worker. I walked into the store and interviewed for the job.

They told me right there that I lacked the experience to be hired. They sent me away with a little more than a hand gesture. My boy could not do shit about it. There I was, shy and discouraged in what I remember for some reason to be a Coogi sweater. I walked out without the job.

I saw Art Van Furniture across the street and walked in with nothing to lose. "I'm not even going to call your references," the interviewer announced with a flourish that she had just discovered an abandoned gold mine. They hired me on the spot as a salesman. Factory men and drug dealers are the "workers" I was brought up on. Not a salesman, but I was being led, so I followed.

With Art Van, I realized that there was a different level of employment. Sales! I started in July. By the time the tax return came, I had made $78k. Everything they gave me to sell ran off the showroom floor. People would ask how I sold so much. I did not have an answer for them at the time. But I now realized that I was the brand, no matter what I was selling. I owned it like none other.

I represented it as a reflection of myself. I found my calling. I was ranked number 12 out of 1200 sales associates in the company. From a sad Coogie sweater to a suit and tie, peacoat, and penny loafers complete with pennies in them, I was the specimen of success.

CHAPTER 2

MY FIRST DRINKS

At my previous job where I took a leap of faith, we had a Hilo driver that could not function without a drink. Everybody knew, but he was high functioning. He would be literally useless around lunchtime. There was a deli on the corner where a lot of the employees would buy lunch. I can honestly say that I have never seen him eat. He would buy two 40s, guzzle them in a matter of minutes, and return to work with newfound energy.

I was a different drinker; I never drank at work but drank two 40s after work. I distinctly remember the cost.

Colt 45 was two for $5. Though I was closeted as a drinker at work, I was unfazed out in the neighborhood. In Detroit, we have a C.R.V. bottle deposit. So, whenever I got broke, I would take two garbage bags full of bottles to the store for the return money. Not proud or embarrassed, just unfazed.

The only references I had of people taking bottles back to the store were kids or crackheads. It is shameful when you are a grown man taking bottles back to buy a drink. But I did not feel shame though. I thought I was unique on the inside even though I was not doing what represented that reality.

I remember one of my uncles would always have a Colt 45 with him whenever he came to visit my cousins. One day, he was so drunk that he held my aunt hostage. I also remember his end. He was found, and he died of liver cirrhosis. And for some reason, he was clutching a rusted ax. My uncle's wife, after he passed, saw me at Mr. C's.

She looked into my trunk and said, "That looks like my husband's trunk."

I got in the car and thought to myself. That's how people see me? That's how I'm living? I didn't stop drinking, but I had that omen of things to come if my drinking habits did not change.

But of course, I didn't listen to myself, my aunt, or anyone else for that matter. My life was on such a high: money, career, and a new car. I was high on the horse. Little did I know that being high on the horse meant the fall would hurt worse. To understand the precursor to my fall, you must understand the beginning of it all.

My First Drink

My boys and I talked about girls and rode bikes. That was what we were thinking about. My best friends had no desire for alcohol or drugs. That was not the scene for kids of a certain age growing up in our neighborhood. I was curious and drank a sip from one of my father's beer cans.

The thought did not enter my mind until I tasted it, but my father would put cigarette butts into old cans, and just my luck, the can that I chose to experiment with was now an ashtray. My mother saw my wrinkled and misshapen face. "That's what you get," she said. She was cool about it because I learned a lesson about drinking. That bitter, ash-paste taste was in my mouth for the longest. My father was a drinker but was not an alcoholic. I thought it was just what grown men did.

I never thought it was something I would do. I hated the smell of my father's or uncle's breath. They smelled like beer. My uncle, the worst example of personal choices, walked into my house when I was eight. I was eating green peas. He stank! "Let me try those," he slurred.

My father told me to share with him from my fork. As soon as he went outside, I went to get another fork. I hated that shit. My two best friends did not have fathers in their houses. One of them thought drinking was cool at a young age.

The negative influence came from him primarily.

His sister sold dope. He was on a different path. One day, on the way to football practice, we saw a six-pack on the other side of a fence in a field. We had no clue how it got there, but it was a new-looking temptation. We each took one, the 4 of us, and opened it.

One by one, we took a sip as the others looked on, anticipating the reaction. My boy who was intoxicated loved it and ended up doing practice somewhat drunk. Of course, we didn't know this at the time, but we all had his back and kept it to ourselves.

After practice, he went back looking for the rest of the beer, and he was instantly turned out. My reaction was different; I sipped it and immediately wanted to spit it out. All I had was a nasty taste in my mouth. I don't pass blame; influences are one thing, but everything that I ever did in my life was my choice, and I know that.

My father was just a reference point for choices I made in my life. I remember telling myself about my father while I was drinking. "He drank two

40s every day and still went to work." I remember referencing him when I was trying to quit. "He quit."

My Second Drink

My sister had just graduated high school, and a couple of my older cousins were celebrating. I hopped in the car with them and headed to Belle Isle Island. Belle Isle was where teenagers from all around Michigan used to hang out, drive around, drink, and just party.

My oldest cousin had a cooler in her van filled with wine coolers. Everybody was drinking; I was the youngest one there. I took a sip of the wine cooler. It didn't taste bad, much different than that nasty taste I got from my father's empty beer can. I liked the taste and could not taste any alcohol.

It was fun in the beginning. I got my first buzz, and it happened fast, not even a full cooler. I waved my hand in front of my face, and it moved faster than I perceived it was moving. It looked like I had four hands. I wanted more of that. I thought it would get better the more I drank, but I was dead wrong. And before I knew it, I was drunk and later got sick. I did not become a drinker at that time. I felt like the experience was whack.

Drinking in Fashion

My friend who took to drinking dropped out of high school because he had a baby, a woman, and a home to manage at 16. He was dabbling in drugs a little, but he drank heavily. Most would say it had to do with father figures or neighborhood influences. I believe it comes down to a personal choice and a vision of yourself.

Drinking is just like fashion. At this point, I had not lost my vision of myself. But drinking is involved in every industry, and it is an industry of its own, so I couldn't hide from it for too long.

It is fashionable. You cannot walk into a party with cheap beer or liquor; people will look at you like a low-rate citizen. Just like a fashion model cannot show up with fake Gucci. But sometimes, you can only buy what you can afford, and where I'm from, most of the time, that was the cheap beer, and we got used to it becoming an acquired taste.

I honestly don't believe that our bodies were designed for drinking anything other than water. Think about it. The first time a baby drinks milk from cows, they will not like it, causing them to throw up. The first time you smoke a cigarette, you cough. The first time you drink pop (by the way, "Pop" is what we call "Soda" in the Midwest), it burns your chest and throat, but you like the taste, and you drink it anyway.

It is the same thing when you drink alcohol; your body gets used to it. It is working on getting the buzz. After a while, your tolerance will increase, and the body is no longer worried about the taste. You are willing to lose friends, livelihood, and more to get the buzz.

Drinking is all about status. I have met people that did not care what they drank as long as they got something to drink. I knew people that would drink rubbing alcohol to get that buzz if they did not have anything else. If I pulled up to an event with my friends drinking Milwaukee's Best, those who drink Remy Martin would clown me. It is the same as showing up to a fashion show with sewn bed sheets.

SECTION II

ORIGIN OF A PROBLEM

CHAPTER 3

WHY I QUIT: PART ONE-SLIM CHANCES

There are reasons you start drinking, and there are reasons you continue. Reasons to continue are called enablers. Enablers can be people, situations, or states of being. For example, popularity is the worst enabler. People give you the benefit of the doubt when you are well known. They buy you drinks because they like to have you around. They want to provide you with excuses for your drinking behaviors and failures. You may try playing "big dog" with your significant others or friends. You become their enabler, or they become your enabler.

People saw me doing dumb shit in my life, but they didn't question the situation. Instead, they would see me and yell, "Where are the 40s at?" As long as you are around that community, they make it alright. You will never quit if that is the case. You must first identify that the person is an enabler. Then get rid of them. If not, you will never quit drinking.

The enabler sees it as help. You are a problem when you are in a bad mood. The person does not want to deal with it. They will tell you, "You need a beer or something." They don't see themselves as the problem. But they are. The enabler comes in various forms. They are mothers, wives, best friends, favorite colleagues, and other close people in your life. Every time they need it, they will come to that enabler. If that person refuses, the alcohol-dependent person will snap at them.

That is why the 12-step program has a step for apologizing to people you have hurt. It is there because we know that it happens. An alcohol-dependent person will only identify alternative options when ready to quit. It does not matter how much they love you; they will look at alcohol as their fix.

It is not until they look at all the havoc and chaos in their lives, the people they have hurt, and the relationships they have damaged that they will find the reason to quit. And that is only when they are ready to leave after seeing the challenge.

The Spiral Downward

I was the guy from our neighborhood who had made it. My $300,000 house was massive. I owned late model cars, flaunted expensive furnishings, and pocketed good money. I was so young that people would ask me if my father was home when they met me at the door of my house.

This time of my life was a transition period like none other. I transitioned from corporate or social drinking to obsessive drinking. The spiral downward was so severe that it seems unreal in retrospect. By 2003, the house and cars were gone.

Fast forward to 2004; now, I lived in a $30,000

house. When the transition was locked in, I was living in an apartment. My home once sported an Italian leather couch, which I kept with me while living in different apartments. In 2004, my friend needed a sofa. I sold him my $4000 couch for $600.

This is what they call "Rock bottom." But I was not ready to give up on drinking. The embarrassment, finances, stature, and other costs had not registered with me yet. When I say it was a downward spiral, I mean no low was low enough for me. I remember one Thanksgiving (before the downfall), particularly well. My house was brand new.

The plan was to have a Thanksgiving get-together at my house with mostly my mother's side of the family. My mother only asked for one accommodation. I had a song dedicated to my late aunt, who had passed away years earlier. "Please don't mention my sister at the party."

She was my favorite aunt. I heard my mom's words as a caution, knowing that mentioning my aunt may trigger others in the family. In my defense, I did not hear her words as a message to me about her. I was drinking all day. My adherence to caution waned steadily. My mother had instructed my brother as well on the prohibition. I knew this because of what happened next. I took control of the music player, turned it off, turned on a camcorder, and read the song I did for my aunt in poem form.

My mother lost it and started crying. My brother and I got into a fight. We ended up on the floor with my mother in the mix. My friend had to break up the fight. Other people came to my mother's aid. It was then that the family knew that something was up with me.

They had to say positive things because I was 20 years old, hosting my entire family in a quarter-million-dollar house purchased with money obtained from nothing illegal. They saw that I had a drinking problem, even among others who were drinking. It was so bad that I thought about that incident even 10 to 15 years after. I regretted it. Still do.

To see my mother crying on the floor was

devastating. I was playing the same two songs on repeat all day. People asked me to change the music, and I would not. I cringe and flood with memories and regret when I hear those songs. This is one of the things that I wish I could change in my life. No one could tell me anything. I had too much power. It wasn't real power, but the administration kept the best advice from me.

My choice was not to heed the positive advice I did receive. I always made choices based on my information and my view of myself. But alcohol distorts those grounded perspectives.

One story illustrates that distortion like no other. I was at work at Art Van when I got paged to the showroom for a phone call. It was my boy, Meech. We call him "Truth." "The White boy said Deangelo's name in a song." That was all that needed to be said, but I still responded with a question. "What?" He repeated it precisely as he had before. "The White boy said Deangelo's name in a song." We both knew what that meant. The "White boy" was a local rapper named Marshal Mathers.

He went by the stage name, "Eminem." I walked across the street to the same Circuit City that I walked in a few years earlier with my Coogi sweater looking for a job. I bought Eminem's first CD. He said it. A tear dropped from my eye. I couldn't help but admit that this guy could rap. I listened to the first five songs, and he referenced my friend again.

Back in the day, we all used to freestyle on the corners all night around that time I used to call myself, "Metro," so I drew a logo and started Metro Records. Back then, we were in our teens, so it wasn't a real company. It was just a name. When I started working in the corporate sales world, being a rapper was put on the back burner.

Truth put Deangelo on the phone, "Do you still have the record company?" Before I could answer, "We have to go after this dude," said Truth.

I knew a producer named Daniel Showers, aka Papa Shane. "If Papa Shane has the same number when I call, it is meant to be." He did. I did not intend to rekindle Metro Records, but that would be the vehicle if we wanted to respond to this perceived disrespect.

After talking with Papa Shane, I called Meech back. We set our sights on the mission. I quit the store, went back to the street, and consumed for the next 15 years with the game and the life. I left the house and everything else, with alcohol as my fuel for every questionable interaction and every regrettable decision.

I was banned from Sony Studios. We got so bad. I woke up the following day and found that I owed $1500 to have the studio cleaned. I had blacked out. What comes with the midpoint is liquid courage. You are fearless in decisions, fighting, and carrying guns. Consequences do not exist. That was my problem. I didn't have that function in my brain.

After all the Eminem drama, my cousins and several friends were hanging out. We were all drunk as fuck. My cousin gave one of my closest friends money to rent his truck for the night. I don't know what my problem was exactly. I was not jealous of the situation. I was more jealous about how he got money to rent the truck. They went into the other room. I took the keys and drove the car 20 miles away. My first cousin was furious the following day.

Moving Out of Favor

When I worked at Art Van, I had a $70k increase in the first six months. I was at $106k for the year. I built a quarter-million-dollar house. I would only drink on the way home and at home. I was no longer on the block acting crazy.

When I got the Eminem call, I knew I would have to leave everything to do what I wanted. I just left. It felt good to let go. Everybody in the studio smoked weed and drank. I knew something was not right.

People would call me and tell me I did something crazy every morning. I moved into another house. My wife filed for divorce and charged me with abandonment. I never went to the court hearings. I didn't see myself happy in that situation, but the drinking had me in a state where I did things the wrong way. If you are not feeling that lifestyle, you sit down and split. You start over if you must. With liquor involved, all the decisions are unhinged and unruly.

People see the damage and the destruction that you create. They see you as a hurricane and fail to see your struggle for happiness. I was searching for a life that was more fun.

At Art Van, I was going to corporate events. I was bored. Drinking was on both sides. But I wanted a lifestyle that was more out there. The corporate mindset was at least on the progressive tip. Street life was more about partying and girls without progress. I still had to wear suits, but I would call into work not wanting to go.

The drinking did not take me out of the routine; the hood did. The people, the environment, and the lifestyle took me down. We had enough money to work with, and the drinking was the fuel. People were following me. I was still the leader that I was. But I was moving out of favor. I had a friend, TJ, who came over to get his haircut at the house that I was staying at, at the time. He was sitting in the chair, and he jumped up when he saw the army of roaches crawling across the wall. He used to come to my big house when I had it. "You left that big ass house for this?" He said. I attempted to deliver a drunken justification, which he rejected. "Nigga, you crazy as fuck!" His voice notified me that I had lost significant points on the basketball court of public opinion. I blew him off.

I was the type of person that would justify my decisions. I told him like I told my other homeboy. I convinced him that the suit and tie life was not me. My mother gave me a specific look that registered her questioning my choices. I responded with that same explanation.

Others questioned as well. Many were engaged in the same lifestyle but had not given up so much. The co-dependent man's method of giving advice would always include some form of the statement like, "Man, you're tripping!" I would tell them, "Don't tell me this when I'm drunk. Tell me when I am sober."

CHAPTER 4

THE BROKE BOYS

Broke Boys was a term I came up with to describe the situation after Art Van. The transition from Art Van in 2004 was a bridge on fire to a rough patch. Drinks and drinkers were always around me. But money was much less plentiful. The cost of the 40s went up.

Milwaukee Best Ice was the secondary option. When you pull up with a much cheaper liquor brand in your hand, you instantly lose status. We embraced the lower level and called ourselves the "Broke Boys."

When the money came back, we were still on the Milwaukee Best. The drinking was at its highest in 2002 – 2007. I went from being the talk of the town and making money to being the subject of town gossip because I no longer cared for the crucial things in life.

My priorities were out of order. I may have convinced myself that I was obsessed with the music, but I was oblivious to my downward spiral. Sometimes, when I sit back and listen to my old music, I can hear the slurring of my words. It's embarrassing to listen to myself sound like my crackhead uncle. The worst part is that my popularity afforded me a pass, and people accepted what I was contributing.

To Make Money

Although I had not reached my drinking slump yet, somehow, I still managed to walk into my life-changing job drunk as fuck on the very first day.

A hangover alone will make you want to stop drinking. I saw coffee and made a b-line for the cups. My logic was undeniable and falsely based on films that suggested that coffee helps sober you up. I drank about 6 cups. I did not gain or retain any information that day. I stood up when they introduced the new hires. I was the third black person hired in their history as a business. I do remember that.

I remember the two others who would go to lunch and drink. One of the guys would keep a fanny pack stocked with mouthwash. As I mentioned that I would not drink during work, I would wait to go to a store on the way home after work. The very first night, I saw the top salesman in the store. "We had a tough day, didn't we?" He reached for his favorite drink. "Yes (I went for mine). We did." This is how my life accelerated with drinking.

It was acceptable in the company I was keeping. I could make money and continue my drinking habit. Keep in mind that drinking is prevalent in my social circles. The line between social disaster and nuts disaster is thin.

The hindrance of alcohol means that you cannot be a specimen. You are destined to be even with others or lower. Yet, I still excelled. This caused me to question what I could do if I stopped drinking. Between this point and the next, I worked hard to conceal my entire ordeal, socially and financially, but the only person that I was fooling was myself.

One of my boys, Lo, knew that I had fallen. He pulled up and asked, "What do you need?" He reached back and gave me money. "What's this for, Lo?" "This is just to get you back on your feet." I knew what time it was. I was so low that he gave me money without asking.

I still remember what I bought: a catfish sandwich and a 40. We went to Chandler Park and sat in the car. We were at the same park as when we were younger.

My favorite cousin was staying with me. He brought some Wild Irish Rose. He walked in with confidence and started yelling, "I got that Ro."

I started drinking it with him because it tasted pretty good. I was drinking it straight from the bottle, not knowing it decreased my credibility. We went to a party. A random guy spotted us and stepped on some rap battle energy. We were not rapping anymore, so I was rusty. Added to that, I was not the best freestyler.

The guy I was battling was better. I was preparing and finding my rhythm, but before I knew it, I blurted out some untamed drunken words and disrespected the guy's girlfriend right in front of him. It was bad. We ran out of the building. We thought it was funny at the time, but I realized my social status was lower for multiple reasons.

My brother is four years younger than me. He would brag about me to all his friends, including his roommate. We went out together, and I could tell that his friend looked up to me. We pulled up to Gratiot and the State Fair. His house was five houses off the corner. I already had a couple of 40s in me. They were weed smokers.

I was acting even more critically because of how they were treating me. I was working to maintain my status, so I smoked weed too. I knew smoking wasn't for me, but I was trying to go with the image they had for me. I was dizzy. I got up and told them I wanted to get some air. I went to the back of my car and threw up intensely. I looked up, and his friend's wife was watching me from the window. I was embarrassed as fuck.

I lived around the corner. I played it off. "Let's go to my house. I need to get something from the crib." I drove down my block and drove past my house. "Ah! I like to drive the other way. That's the only reason I missed it." I busted a U-turn and went back down my street. I missed the house again. Drove right past it.

"What? You all distracting me." My brother was looking at me funny by this time. I passed the house again. My brother couldn't take any more of the dumb shit, so he spoke up, "Pull over the car." "Bro, y'all should not have had me smoking the weed!" I attempted to save face. I went from the top when I met his friend to the bottom by the night's end. You know when people are looking up to you. You also know when they are feeling the opposite.

There is no way that I can throw up in his driveway, drive past my house three times, and still save face. I should not have been driving in the first place. Even with the drunken episodes and embarrassing nights out, I still influenced my younger family members.

One of my cousins grew up a Jehovah's Witness. As he got older, he moved away from that religion altogether. In that religion, they were not allowed to hang around worldly people, and I was as worldly as they get. So, we weren't as close as I was with some of my other cousins; I have about 100 first cousins, by the way (another story).

One day, we saw each other at Art Van while I working. This was right around the timeframe when I decided to make music instead of being an employee. He fell right in with the drinking and the music. Drinking was so much of a big deal that he bought a black sub-urban and pimped it out with a full bar. He was working at Chrysler, so he had money to blow, and that's exactly what he did. He blew it. He pulled up with a bar in the back of the truck.

When I say bar, I mean he had tubes professionally installed with multiple types of liquor on a spout. He even had the fancy glasses that he would put in the cup holder and press one of the three buttons that he had installed, matching whatever liquor he had in the back, and it would pour the liquor into his glass just like a real bar. I felt somewhat responsible. I made drinking so acceptable that he wasted $30k on his truck.

At the time, we were impressed. Looking back with a sober mind, it is some of the dumbest shit we ever did. If he had been pulled over, it would have been an automatic D.U.I. But you know what's funny? He has zero D.U.I.s. I wish I could say the same, but unfortunately, I have three, with the third one being a felony.

When you drink, you think people can't see your flaws. You are riskier as a result. I did so much because I didn't know people could see it. I'm speaking specifically of my lowest point of drinking i.e. 2004, which might seem weird to you because I didn't get my second D.U.I. until 2007. And I didn't quit drinking until 2010. Although D.U.I.s are a pretty good sign that there is a problem, I knew well before that, especially in 2004.

At this time, I was drinking Remy Martin founded

by Paul-Emile Remy in the 1700s. This family business was passed along to his grandson after his death.

Remy is on the higher end of the popularity charts when it comes to status. In other words, it's not cheap, and I made a lot of money at that time by selling burnout phones to street dudes.

For the uninitiated, these phones burn out in about 40 days, and I hit $400 on each phone, but they did not want them long-term because of their business. We called them "Bernie Macs" before Metro P.C.S came and shut it down. I was so official with it that I put a huge light-up T-Mobile sign in my garage and sold them like crack.

This hustle lasted about three months before I was back on the couch drinking E&J. Another brand named after its creators, Brothers Ernest and Julio Gallo, which has a net worth of 12 billion dollars. I could get into how fucked that is, giving that most people that drink this are of lower social status, but I will just stick to my story.

Drinking E&J was the liquor version of "Broke

Boys."

My cousin and his boy came up with the idea to have a car wash. We went down to the corner where there was an empty old car lot.

What I was drinking at that time was important because it showed the status switch after the fall of the Bernie Mac business. The idea for the car wash was certainly alcohol-fueled. My sales background made me cocky. Plus, I was drunk and feeling invincible. I said, "Let's get some girls. And, that's not enough. Let's sell hotdogs." The girls were half naked. "Sex sells, right?" I was dressed like I was going to the club; I mean, I looked like I was about to rap on stage or something. That was day number one.

By the 4th day of this ghetto-ass car wash, I was in the same clothes. My cousin pulled me aside and said, "Bro, you're looking bad." It was not only the clothes but the fact that I had not showered. Keep in mind that the girl I was with was a heavy drinker too, and she wasn't bringing it to my attention. So in my mind, I was good, but I was wrong. I was musty and smelled like straight liquor.

I usually didn't like being the guy with breath so foul that people turned their heads. But alcohol had me, and drinking was more important. "You can tell?" I was exposed. It didn't register to me that my cover was blown. I thought that no one could see me and what I was doing. "Bro, you're raw! You've been wearing the same clothes for four days."

It wasn't just a financial challenge that I needed to overcome. The problem was quickly escalating into bankruptcy of character. I could see the demise, but I was a moviegoer, looking at the screen with no way to order the actors. I wanted to yell, cut, reset, or some other direction to regain control of the situation. I was powerless at that moment because alcohol tied my hands behind my back and removed my voice.

CHAPTER 5

WHY I QUIT -PART TWO: SHADY CHARACTER

I was going through a lot between 2004 and 2005. This is where you, as the reader, can learn something. There was a point when I was driving while drinking. I was conscious enough to recognize the danger in my actions but gone sufficient to be pleading within myself. "You are drinking too much. Nigga, you trippin."

I constantly compared my sober self to my non-sober self. I felt like I was one of the ones who made it. My friends were concerned that I had lost what I had achieved and was going lower than I had. I knew it at the moment, but I hid behind the wall I perceived. I thought people could not see everything that was going on.

When you are drunk, you think you are fooling everyone. That deception is the admission to yourself that you are tripping. There is nothing you will be able to find in a book or from another human being that will instantly fix your drinking problem.

There is no magic potion, no unique remedy, and not even a prayer that can improve your drinking problem; only you can.

Self and the Need to Quit

You know that you have done things that you should not have done. You may not feel you need to quit because you want to be a specimen. You only desire to leave because you want to stop doing unsustainable things. Let me tell you point blank that if you have never explored who you are, you can never know who you are to be. You must respond to your internal authenticity. No one can tell you what you need to be.

Someone can tell you what you should not have done. They can describe the illegality or the harm you caused. But they can never communicate who you are. If you have walked around with a void, absent sense of self, you don't have a direction to turn in after drinking.

Creating an additional void by letting go of addiction will make relapse more often. You must have a sense of yourself that is solid and well-formed. You must know who you are. If you don't see that person, you may be lost. Your friends must be able to point you in the direction of you—you that is solid, self-aware, productive, and progressive. If you don't have that sense of self, work toward that reality.

My whole battle was between the "me I knew" and the "me I was acting out." I did not need anything more than myself to make the change toward sobriety. I brag that I quit alone, but that is not a brag. It worked for me to get back to myself. If you cannot find yourself and you are attempting to quit drinking, at that point, you need to rely on what is presented or court-ordered for you. You must go before the group, state your name, and humiliate yourself. You must attend the classes. You must find yourself in the process and respond to the process. Beyond this is the worst step. The drastic action is in-house treatment or rehab. The step after that is death. And there are multiple ways to get to that step—cirrhosis of the liver, drunk driving accidents, murder, and more.

The turning point is identifying that alcoholism is a disease, and diseases kill. They can either kill you or even worse; you can kill innocent people by getting behind the wheel drunk. Someone once told me that going to prison for the rest of your life for killing somebody with your car is not the most innovative way to get sober. This is what we must prevent.

Additionally, I remember my mother asked me one day when I was about to leave her house after drinking. "So, you just aren't gonna stop drinking until you kill somebody, huh?" My mother was indeed my angel on earth, so much so that the incident of that Thanksgiving Day stuck with me forever.

Mother's Memory & Quitting

My mother was a housewife. My father worked at Chrysler. She made sure we went to Mr. C's and had two 40s of Budweiser in the refrigerator when my father came home each day. Back in the day, we had a Chrysler imperial with a big bench seat in the front, and she would sit hip to hip with my father. He would have the beer while he drove to my grandmother's house for our weekly visits.

He would grab another tall boy on the way home. That's what he called it. My father was mean as fuck! But we wanted nothing. Without going into specifics, my mother wanted something different for us. She wanted us to be good kids and sincerely expressed her disapproval of men hitting women to me and my brother, and if we ever put our hands on a woman, she would not be on our side at all.

She told us that our grandmother told my father the same thing. It was also crucial that family vices stayed private. One day, I got into an argument with someone on the corner. I had my cousin's gun. He had given it to me to hold. My mother found it before I had a chance to use it.

She had taken the bullets out at Thanksgiving in my big house. "Dream" is a poem about my aunt. My mother asked me not to mention it, but I read the poem aloud. These were the things that my mother remembered. I had moved to a small house in Detroit when she developed congestive heart failure. Our communications during that period were intentionally heartfelt. My heart was heavy regarding the pain that I had put her through.

Seeing myself and my actions through her eyes was sobering in many ways. I want to say that her point of view helped me to quit. But quitting is not about how others perceive you. Even a mother's stare doesn't penetrate the fortress of will, practice, and self-deception. As her illness progressed, I saw my illness for what it was.

Alcoholism was suffocating as well. Yet, I was focused on what I could still accomplish rather than what I was incapable of. My mom entered the hospital on an unremarkable day toward the end of the week. She passed away five days later.

I remember because I was pulled over for driving while intoxicated in a borrowed car just a day before she was admitted. I found out later that shotguns, ski masks, and other robbery supplies were in the car trunk.

Between the D.U.I. and the contraband in the car, they would have thrown my ass in jail. I would have missed my mother's passing if I had been incarcerated. Instead, I was let go with a warning. It was a mixture of the policemen knowing what Detroit was and how I talked to the police officers. Plus, I am highly favored. I know I have a higher calling.

Computer Store Business

As I said, I was still excelling beyond what the typical man from my background could obtain. That supported my drinking as a secondary activity. Yet, I was beginning to have thoughts that shook my confidence.

I opened my first computer store in 2009. What was happening was that my image was not me. I was accepting the conversations about me. I laughed, but I soon realized that people were not laughing with me. They were laughing at me. I knew that the persona was not me. I knew my body needed the buzz, but my reputation was suffering. This was after everyone saw my complete demise. I was not the manager. I owned everything in the store. I taught myself how to fix computers.

I was still drinking, but I was back to moving forward and progressing upward. I owned two computer stores during my drinking days! That's not a small accomplishment. I would go to the 7/11 around the corner to buy E and J V.S.O.P. I would have a Big Gulp cup and fill it with liquor. I would drink behind the counter during my work in the store. One of my friends stopped by to buy some things. After looking around for a few moments, he asked, "Why did you open a computer store?" "I did it, so I could drink on the job!" I responded with a laugh, knowing on some level that my response was more honest than jest. I expected him to congratulate me on the positives and the negatives.

He did. "That's what's up!" I am sure that he knew about what I had been through. He was there for the downfall. But, by that time, I was in a BMW. I was not supposed to be driving, but I owned a 750. I am also sure that he wanted to check me in some way for the downfall. But he could not.

I was doing well in defiance of the predictions and the penal system. I eventually quit while I was working there. That story is for another chapter, but the experience was a slow burn toward a realization. Buy, sell, and trade was an opportunity. I did not know at the time that you needed a license and registration from the sheriff.

Someone came in to check to see if an iPad that was stolen was in my store. It happened that one of those I had accepted for pawns was stolen. I remember a group of kids would come and hang out at the store. They were all cool with me, and they thought it was funny that I was drinking on the job.

One time, a kid went behind the counter and took an iPod that he claimed was his. I snapped at him in a significant way; I embarrassed him in front of his friends, called him a bitch, and threatened him. He was terrified. I felt bad for him because he did not know the demons in me that could be released for minor reasons. But it was too late, the bad thing is that I felt powerful at the time going off on him, but the next day, I felt like shit! And that's when I was like, "You have two computer stores, but you are drunk as fuck every day, imagine what you could accomplish in this world if you were sober."

When you have a business, you must have particular business etiquette, no matter what. For me, to go there was messy. I was not satisfied with myself. I began to talk with myself like I did back in 2004. "The owner of this business will not be drunk again." "This is how this business will be run." I always spoke to customers and wondered if they could smell the liquor.

My father always told me, "If you can ask the question, the answer is in the question." I looked down between my feet where I sat the Big Gulp. I was moving away from the idea of drinking as a routine. I started asking myself, "How did I feel when I was younger? What was my mental state? How do I get my mental state back to that?" It took years to figure out. I listened to others talk about me. I witnessed my significant fall through the eyes of others while attempting to live my best life.

SECTION III

D.U.I. (DRIVING UNDER THE INFLUENCE) STORIES

CHAPTER 6

MY STORIES OF D.U.I

Driving under the influence (D.U.I.) is the penal system's designation for drinkers who dare to get behind the wheel of a motor vehicle and get caught. Often, getting seen is due to additional moving violations like swerving, wrecking, or causing an accident. My stories of D.U.I. offer a view into the system and a progression of my maturity and sobriety. In addition to those personal elements, I see a system that increasingly works to degrade and dehumanize.

First D.U.I.

I was working at the dealership. I was still at the big house. My brother was staying with me. He had a newborn at the time. He had an ice-cold 40 in my refrigerator. Remember that my brother was not a drinker; I genuinely believe he was only drinking because I was. Knowing this, I drank his beer, intending to replace it, but he got home before I could.

We made a run to the store just four blocks away. We entered the store and picked out two 40s from the cold case. On the way home, I ran out of gas in a brand-new Jeep. The police came up behind me. My thought was one of relief. "Help at a moment's notice," I thought. "Thank you, officer. We've run out of gas." I prided myself in how I talked with officers and was always able to de-escalate situations, even getting out of tickets. "Have you been drinking?" This officer was not into pleasantries. "Yes. Hours ago. Can you push me to—?" He cut me off as my presumption of his assistance faded. "Let me have your license and registration."

The next several minutes were a cautionary tale about police stops in neighborhoods with a particular skin hue. He came back and was rude. He searched the car and found the 40. He put me in handcuffs and wrote on the ticket that I was drinking and driving. "Why did you write D.U.I. when we have been on the side of the road for 45 minutes?" He took the ticket from me and wrote that he saw us pull to the side of the road, right in front of me.

My first D.U.I., and I was not even driving. I had to spend the night in jail. Even worse, I was driving a company car from the dealership that I thought they were going to fire my ass the next day, but that's when I found out that all my coworkers had D.U.I.s. I went to the phone book to find a D.U.I. lawyer. He charged me $1800. That was my second lesson on the ills of the system—all that money to appear with me in court. The judge in court gives me a $500 fine, and that is all. Another expense that seemed out of proportion with the alleged crime. But I was grateful. A slap on the wrist, and I was released. "Don't do it again." A year later, the same judge got a D.U.I. himself.

My second D.U.I. stop did not result in a ticket or any reprimand. I was shooting dice at the corner store. I lost all my money, so I borrowed a friend's car to go back home to get a check to cash.

My house was one house off the corner. It was 2 am, so I wasn't trying to sit at a red light too long, so I ran the light and turned left. As soon as I turned, I saw the disco lights; the police were behind me. Instead of stopping, I pulled into my driveway and walked out like it wasn't me. But the police pull right behind me. The neighbors came out gawking at the commotion of police lights. I told the cops that I ran the light because people were out trying to rob me. He allowed me to continue into the house while he checked my license and registration. He greeted me when I came out of the house with two comments. He told me, "Stop drinking and driving. And you have a child support warrant." I go back to the spot, bragging about my finesse.

The friend I borrowed the car from looked at me as crazy. I thought he was looking at me because he thought I had fucked up his car. He didn't speak; he just looked at me and told me to follow him to his car. I followed him outside, got to the driver's door, opened it, reached under the seat, and pulled out a fully loaded Glock 40 with one in the head. I just put my head down. Then he walked me around to his trunk. He had gloves and a mask in his trunk. This dude had a complete robbery kit in his trunk. I did not know he was a stickup kid.

At that time, Detroit was handing out mandatory two years sentences for possessing any guns. No questions asked. Not to mention if that gun was dirty, which it probably was.

I had another run-in that resulted in a court date. I was at a club on Seven Mile Road. I was over the top drunk. I left and ran a red light on purpose in a brand-new Chrysler 300. I almost got hit by a couple of cars, and the police saw this. I tried to do the same thing as I had before. I told the police that I was being chased. They were not buying it.

The wait for my appearance in court was unremarkable, but I remember a moment in the hallway, ready to go into the courtroom. A bailiff pulled me aside. He said, "Do you have $500? I will make it go away for $500." Standard operating procedure for a full court docket, I later found out. No lawyer. No $1800 additional charge. He showed me the expunged record with the reduced reckless driving charge before my exit. He was true to his word. He made it go away.

Second D.U.I.

My second D.U.I. was the one I didn't give any resistance to. I knew I was wrong. I got out of the car and complied 100% with the police officers. But it was also the D.U.I. that I learned that the system of licensed bars and the government might be out to get you. I'll get to that later. It was 2007; my rap group and some of my cousins went out to celebrate my sister's birthday. We drank all night, and by the end of the night, I was drunk as fuck! We all were; I remember my sister asked me if I was okay to drive, and I insisted, I was.

I made a right-hand turn in the wrong direction, and as soon as my tires hit the main road, the police were right there. All they did was turn their lights on. I was arrested, and my car was impounded. I had to hire a lawyer. This time, it wasn't $1800.00. It was more like $18,000. It was the weekend, so I could not bond out until the following Monday.

After that, I went on a serious mission to quit, and I did okay, but I eventually fell off the wagon. I want to make another point. When I got my first D.U.I., I received a slap on the wrist, and I never learned anything about alcoholism or the havoc it could cause. I just paid the fine and walked out of the court. If I had been given any penalty on the first one, I might not have ever gotten the second one and of course, never got the third one.

The Third D.U.I., I Quit.

I was officially off the sauce. I'm not sure how long I was clean and sober, but it was long enough to make a relapse feel like a letdown. I was still working at the dealership. We had a going away party at the strip club for our sales manager. He hooked everybody up with brand new cars, and he had just helped me get a brand-new Chrysler Aspen. I didn't know that it was a target.

After the second D.U.I., they took the license plate from my car and forced me to have a paper license. This is another way that they identify those with suspended or restricted rights. They allow you only to drive to work.

The party was at Cheetah's on Eight Mile Road, and the peer pressure from the people I was around was too much. I got my Diet Coke; people were laughing. I looked at a shot of Hennessey and thought I could do that and go home. I did four shots and decided to go home. I got a little buzz. I was driving down the street and saw the police car. I tried to play it cool. I pulled into the parking lot of a store and got out. They knew what it was because of the paper license plate. They came up behind me and asked if I was drinking. I refused the breathalyzer, so they took me to the hospital and drew blood.

I thought I could get the girl to throw away the record, still convinced that my silver tongue could work wonders. No dice. The arresting officer had a message for me as he was processing me. "I have never booked someone for D.U.I. that was sober." I was sober, but I was stuck since the blood alcohol level was higher than the allowable limit. He continued, "This is a felony." "A felony!" All I could do was exclaim, repeating his words.

By the sentencing for the second D.U.I., I was up for a third. My lawyer postponed the second so that I could simultaneously stand for the second and third. The judge was talking down to me. He saw the real second D.U.I. on the record, but it looked as if it wasn't thrown out. He could not act on it but spoke to me like this was my fourth instance.

He made me look like the lowest person on the planet. I was still defiant. "You're looking at a few moments of my life on paper and judging me based on that." He would not let up. He asked me how often I was drinking and driving, and I paused. "Is it that bad that you had to pause?" He continued to go at me. He was so tough and animated that people in the courtroom were laughing.

Luckily, he would not be the judge to sentence me because the third D.U.I. was a felony, so it was a higher court. I got sentenced by an Oakland

County Circuit Judge for the second and third. Both carried the same penalty. I was drinking peach vodka the night before my hearing, and I had no fear. My lawyer was a black woman whose husband had a drinking problem. So, she could tell by looking at me that I had been drinking, and she confronted me.

I responded, "Now, why would I come to the court drunk on a D.U.I. charge." I knew I had put her in a bad situation. She was not prepared to defend me in that state. The person in front of me was jailed for the same charge, which made me nervous, but I also felt like that, as I didn't want to get hit with the same charge as that guy before me. That was all on me.

I chose to speak up for myself and appealed to the sensibility of the judge. "If I were sober, I would have never driven drunk." My lawyer looked at me like I was the dumbest person alive. "In other words, …" I turned and looked at the clock (A trick that I learned in theater class. Look at the clock and the audience will think that you are looking at them.). "I did not know that drinking was a disease.

This should be added to the curriculum of all schools in America so that our kids are educated. And if there is anyone in this courtroom that was an issue with drinks or suffers from the disease of alcoholism, take it from me, you don't have to die from this. On my first, I got a slap on the wrist. Secondly, I received great information." I turned back to the judge. To my lawyer's amazement, the judge was lenient. I received a 45-day work release. And for the first time, the long hours at the dealership were appreciated.

There was a body scanner that scans each inmate before entering the jail. If that goes off, you go straight to prison. Medication and even mouthwash will set this machine off. I met several people from diverse walks of life in the jail. One dude was convicted of insurance fraud. He was not like me. When I am forced to be sober, I don't crave liquor. This guy had a year's work release with a 10-year charge over his head. He came back to the jail one day drunk. He was not just drunk. He was drunk as fuck! He wasn't even there for a D.U.I charge, and he probably didn't even have a drinking problem, but drinking will fuck up your life even when it is not your problem.

We all felt bad for him. We knew what he was giving up. As he was handcuffed, I remember the look on his face. It was the saddest shit ever. I believe even the police officers booking him felt bad.

Under Michigan State laws, a fourth D.U.I. will send you to prison for one year.

This is another reason I quit drinking. I knew the only way to ensure I didn't get a fourth D.U.I. was not to drink at all. I was pulled over on two other occasions where I was let go and not charged. I hate to say it, but both times, I was drunk. The first one happened one day after work; a coworker had a small get-together at her house. She did not have my beer of choice. I believe it was Molson Ice.

After a few hours of drinking, she offered kittens to all of us. If I was sober, there's no way I would have accepted a cat. But being drunk, I took one with me and headed home, driving down Eight Mile Rd. Eight Mile is a road that divides the suburbs from the city. One side is Detroit, and the other is East Point. The East Point police were right behind me and pulled me over. There's a hump on the road, and if you drive fast enough, it elevates you.

I remembered a myth floating around the neighborhood back in the day that if you put a penny in your mouth, it would throw off the breathalyzers. Me believing this bullshit, I took a cup holder full of pennies and threw them in my mouth. I also put the kitten on my lap. The police officer approached the car and asked for my registration and driver's license. He noticed the cat and asked me where I was coming from, and I told him I had rescued it. He said, "This late at night! You're out rescuing cats. I've heard it all step out of the car." This was my first time being pulled over while I was drunk, so I was scared as fuck!

At that moment, his shoulder radio went off with a code of 187. He heard it. He hesitated. He looked at me and returned to his car to answer the call. When he came back to my car, he said, "It's your lucky fucking day. I suggest you spit the pennies out and get your ass home." Feeling invincible, I spit the pennies out, put the cat in the back seat, and drove with two hands all the way home. The good thing is that I lived on West Eight Mile, so it was only a few miles away.

The second time was very similar to the previous time. I was coming from the suburbs, and again I was drunk as fuck, driving down Dequindre Rd. I fell asleep behind the wheel. When I woke up, a telephone pole was in front of me. I swerved and missed it. This scared the shit out of me. I was still drunk. I tried my best to straighten up and drive straight, but I kept dozing off; it seemed like every other minute. Of course, I was pulled over. This part is gonna sound unbelievable, but it's the truth.

The officer's radio goes off when I'm out of my car. I didn't hear the code or anything like the other time, but I swear he said almost identical to what the other officer said to me on Eight Mile Rd. "Today is your lucky day. Get home!" Looking back now, I could have killed myself or innocent people and changed so many people's lives in one split second. So, when I say I'm highly favored, I'm not saying I'm highly favored because I got away with drinking and driving, I'm highly favored because I didn't kill myself or anyone else. I'm still here to write this book. I could have kept these two stories out of this book, but I wanted to prove a point.

Before I get into more of my stories, I would like to make another point. As I look back and analyze the people I was around and those that got D.U.I.s, they all said this statement, including me, "I got caught drinking and driving." And that's just what it is, caught. Think of how many times you got away with it; I know that I've driven drunk hundreds of times. Drinking and driving is serious because you automatically turn your car into a weapon of mass destruction. A murdering machine in a sense, but there are other ways that drinking could fuck up lives.

Drug use and alcoholism have always been

associated with the lower class, middle class, and especially, the invisible class. But let's be clear, celebrities and athletes develop severe alcohol and drug problems as well. Drinking can cause homelessness and even cause you to lose your job or a multi-million-dollar contract from the N.F.L. or the N.B.A. And like any other disease, alcoholism knows no race, class, or sex, and it affects everyone in all walks of life.

CHAPTER 7

STORIES OF SOME CELEBRITIES {I}

D.U.I. Stories of Andre Benjamin: How It Affected Him and How He Got Sober

A hip-hop recording artist and actor, Andre Benjamin, oozes creativity in his fashion, wordplay, and, most notably, his music. Over the years, the young man has been known on stage, screen, and radio as Andre 3000.

Andre Lauren Benjamin was born in Atlanta, Georgia, on May 27, 1975, to Sharon Benjamin, a young single mother who raised him to be clean-cut and preppy. She noted Benjamin's uncanny response to music and sounds when he was still an infant. She once said, "The things that babies play with, he would not play with. You would just put him on the blanket and give him some newspaper, and he will just take the paper and crumble it; he loved the sounds."

At age 16, Benjamin began to rebel against the authority of his mother and let his grades drop. His mother sent him to live with his father, Lawrence Walker, a collections agent. Benjamin's father turned out to be more of a buddy than an authority, and Benjamin spent more time at clubs and parties than at school.

We can trace this to the beginning of his becoming addicted to alcohol due to his early exposure. He dropped out of school in his junior year but later earned his high-school equivalency.

His career soon took off with his friend, Patton. The duo, now Outkast, contributed to a Christmas album with its first single. The song, "Players' Ball," which laments the shortage of Christmas cheer in the ghetto, went gold and held the number-one spot on the rap charts for six weeks in 1993.

Benjamin and Patton chose the name "Outkast" as a description of their artistic intent. The spelling is a reference to the dictionary pronunciation script for "Outcast," defined as "homeless" or "not accepted in society."

Music reviewers labeled their musical style as a new sound called "Dirty South" hip-hop. Yet, commentators have consistently praised Outkast for creating music that defies categorization. As self-imposed social outcasts, they have sought to showcase each artist's unique perspective of the world.

Each track was an experiment in American sound-blend. Though varied in beat, rhythm, instrumentation, and melodic theme, Outkast's Benjamin and Patton have tagged their work as "Slumadelic." They consider their lyrics as positive messages about real stories of American life.

Andre 3000 may experiment with bow ties and

suspenders, but he became someone who does not toy with alcohol and drugs. Word has it that Ice Cold has not touched a mind-altering substance for nearly two decades. Andre decided to make the change after partying too hard in his younger days. He told VIBE in 2012, *"I looked in the mirror and saw myself deteriorating, and I was like, 'Man, we are doing too much, way too much.' So, I decided to go for A.A. and decided to stop this addiction."* Along with being sober, Andre 3000 has also been a vegetarian for nearly two decades.

It has been a while since Andre 3000 has last smoked kush. When they cut their first album, *Southernplayalisticadillacmuzik,* Benjamin decided to abstain from drinking, smoking, and consuming meat and dairy products. At the same time, he began to dress more eccentrically.

LESSONS FROM ANDRE 3000'S LIFESTYLE

1. He cleaned up real good

The first lesson we can take from Andre 3000 is that it is possible for anyone to become sober, even celebrities. Andre 3000 was able to change his lifestyle and achieve sobriety despite having a party-oriented background. The dude was tearing it up in the Atlanta club scene before he decided to get clean.

Cleaning up your act is possible no matter who you are or what your background is. I've heard it said that the first step is admitting that you have a problem. Andre 3000 did just that when he looked in the mirror and saw himself "deteriorating." He realized that he had a problem and needed to make a change.

Cleaning up has its challenges, but it is possible. The key is to take it one day at a time and to surround yourself with a supportive community. I mean folks who are going to help you stay on the straight and narrow, not enable you to keep partying. That's why Andre 3000 went to A.A. meetings. He needed support from people who understood what he was going through.

2. Andre 3000's story is a reminder that sobriety is a lifelong journey

Andre 3000 has been sober for over two decades now, but he didn't achieve sobriety overnight. It was a long and difficult journey for him, and it's something that he continues to work on every day.

This is a reminder that sobriety is not a destination that you reach and then never have to think about again. It's a lifelong journey that requires effort and commitment. If you're struggling with addiction, know that help is available and recovery is possible. The only way to achieve sobriety is to take it one day at a time; I mean you wanna be like Andre 3000, don't you? Then get to it!

Take that, haters! Andre 3000 is sober, successful, and still making great music. If he can do it, anyone can.

3. Early exposure to alcohol can lead to addiction

Andre 3000's story is also a reminder that early alcohol exposure can lead to addiction. He started drinking and smoking at a young age, and it quickly spiraled out of control.

If you're a parent, this is something to keep in mind. You may think it's harmless to let your kids have a few sips of your beer or a puff of your cigarette, but it can be a slippery slope. It's best to just keep alcohol and tobacco out of the house altogether if you have kids.

Kids are impressionable, and they're more likely to develop addictions if they start using substances at a young age. So, if you want to avoid having an alcoholic or addict in your family, it's best to just keep the booze and drugs away from the kiddos.

As a dad, I can attest to this. My kids are not allowed to have any alcohol or tobacco, and I make sure to keep all those substances out of the house. It's just not worth the risk. Although I've messed up a time or two when my kids saw me in complete drunkenness or smoking a blunt, I had to have a talk with them afterward and let them know that what they saw me doing was not okay and that I was working on changing my ways. These scenarios were definitely teachable moments for me as a father, and I'm grateful that I corrected my mistakes before it was too late.

4. **You can still have fun without alcohol or drugs**

Just because Andre 3000 is sober doesn't mean he doesn't know how to have a good time. He's proof that you can still enjoy life without alcohol or drugs.

If you're struggling with addiction, know that there is life after recovery. You don't have to give up all your fun activities just because you're sober. In fact, you might find that you enjoy them even more without the help of substances. I put it to you guys, "Is it really that much fun to be hungover or high all the time?" To me, it sounds like more of a drag. But hey, that's just me.

Of course, early alcohol exposure is not the only factor that can lead to alcohol addiction. There are many other factors, including mental health and social factors. However, this is an important reminder that we need to be careful about the messages we're sending to our kids about alcohol.

Let's face it, the media glorifies drinking and partying, and it's easy for kids to get the wrong idea about what's acceptable behavior. We need to be careful about the messages we're sending to our kids about alcohol and other substances.

The bottom line is that sobriety is a journey, not a destination. It's something that you have to work on every day. If you're struggling with addiction, know that you are not alone and that help is available. Recovery is possible, and there is life after addiction. Just ask Andre 3000.

5. It is possible to overcome addiction and live a sober lifestyle

The life of a celebrity is often one of excess. They have more money than they know what to do with, and they often party hard to blow off steam. As a result, many celebrities have struggled with addiction at some point in their lives.

With my experience and as evident in Andre 3000's and others' stories, I can confidently say drunkenness does not have to be a part of your life if you don't want it. It is possible to overcome addiction and live a sober lifestyle. Being sober does not mean you have to be boring. In fact, you might find that you enjoy life more without the help of substances.

It's a game of choice my friend. You can either choose to be a slave to your addiction, or you can choose sobriety. The choice is yours. Just as we have the choice to pick up a drink or drug, we also have the choice to put it down and never pick it up again. Just like Andre 3000, I have chosen sobriety. And I'm never looking back.

6. Sober lifestyles can be healthy and successful

Addiction is a serious issue, and it's important to remember that sobriety is the only way to overcome addiction. However, it's also important to remember that sober lifestyles can be healthy and successful. This is something that Andre 3000 has proven. Andre is proof that you can live a sober lifestyle and still be successful. The dude has been sober for years and is still one of the most successful rappers in the game. Success has nothing to do with drinking or doing drugs. Although the society we live in today would have you believe otherwise.

D.U.I. Stories of Brad Pitt

William Bradley "Brad" Pitt (born December 18, 1963) is an American actor and film producer. Pitt has received two Academy Award nominations and four Golden Globe nominations, winning one.

Pitt began his acting career with television guest appearances, including a role on the CBS prime-time soap opera *Dallas* in 1987. He later gained recognition as the cowboy hitchhiker who seduces Geena Davis's character in the 1991 road movie *Thelma & Louise*. He has been described as one of the world's most attractive men, a label for which he has received substantial media attention. Pitt owns a production company named "Plan B Entertainment," whose productions include the 2007 Academy Award-winning Best Picture, *The Departed*.

Pitt is well known for his dedication to environmental issues, including sustainable housing projects. He has also been a longtime supporter of same-sex marriage, famously saying in 2006 that he would marry then-girlfriend Angelina Jolie once same-sex marriage was legalized in America.

Brad is also famous for his high-profile relationships with famous women, including Jolie (to whom he was married from 2014 – 2019) and Jennifer Aniston (to whom he was married from 2000 – 2005).

Since beginning his relationship with Jolie, he has become increasingly involved in social issues both in the United States and internationally.

It was reported in 2019 that the actor spent a year and a half in Alcoholics Anonymous after Angelina Jolie filed for divorce in 2016. He said, *"I had taken things as far as I could take, so I removed my drinking privileges."*

How He Became Addicted to Alcohol

Back in his stoner days, he had wanted to smoke a joint with Jack, Snoop, and Willie. He could not even remember when he got started. Since he got out of college, there was no day he was not having booze, a spliff, or any other thing. He once spoke in an interview that he was a stoner who gets these idiotic ideas. Though he didn't want to indict the others, he made others do things except for Willie.

He had two credits short of graduating college, so he decided to drop out. He said, *"All I had to do was write a paper. What kind of guy is that? That guy scares me. The guy who always leaves a little on his plate. For a long time, I thought I did too much damage—drugs and alcohol damage. I was a bit of a drifter. A guy who felt he grew up in something of a vacuum and wanted to see things and wanted to be inspired. I followed that other thing. I spent years faking off alcohol, but then I got burnt out and felt that I was wasting my opportunity. It was a conscious change."*

His past alcohol addiction, according to one of his discussions with former Legends of the Fall and Meet Joe Black co-star Anthony Hopkins in a December 2019 Interview magazine chat. He said, *"I just saw it as a disservice to myself, as an escape."*

Pitt told GQ Style in 2017, several months after Angelina Jolie, with whom he shares six kids, filed for divorce. Even till the previous year, he was still finding it hard to deal with things. He said, *"I was boozing too much. I realized that a lot of cigarettes were my pacifiers, but I was running from feelings. It just became a problem, and I am pleased it's been half a year, which is bittersweet, but I've got my feelings at my fingertips again. I think that's part of the human challenge: You either deny them all of your life or answer them and evolve."*

How He Became Sober

He, first, gave credit to Bradley Cooper. He said this about Bradley Cooper after he presented him with an award at the 2020 National Board of Review.

Quitting Pot and Alcohol and Overcoming Pot Addiction

He got sick of himself at the end of the 1990s and had to hide from the celebrity thing. He was smoking too much, and he would sit on the couch turning into a doughnut. The actor acknowledged he got irritated with himself and thought, *"What's the point? I know better than this."*

He said that after a trip to Casablanca, Morocco, in the mid-to-late 1990s, where he witnessed a lot of poverty and sick children, he "just quit," adding, *"I stopped grass then, I mean, pretty much and decided to get off the couch."*

Hiding Out

"I spent the '90s trying to hide out, trying to duck the full celebrity cacophony," Pitt told Parade magazine in 2011. *"I started to get sick of sitting on a couch, holding a joint, and hiding out. It started feeling pathetic. It became obvious to me that I was intent on trying to find a movie about an interesting life, but I wasn't living an interesting life myself. I think that my marriage [to Jennifer Aniston] had something to do with it. Trying to pretend the marriage was something that it wasn't."*

Motivation to Quit Marijuana

The actor said on Real Time with Bill Maher in 2009 that he quit marijuana when he had kids. He and his ex-wife Angelina Jolie are parents of six. He said, "*I'm a dad now. You want to be alert.*" This newfound happiness was hard-won.

In a new profile from The New York Times, the actor revealed that he is now sober after spending some time in recovery with Alcoholics Anonymous. His tumultuous divorce from Angelina Jolie came as a shock to many when it was announced in 2016 that their eleven-year relationship would come to an end.

At the time, rumors circulated about why the two would split after over a decade with six kids in the mix. Still, it was reported that one catalyst for the divorce proceedings had something to do with Pitt's drinking. "*I had taken things as far as I could take it, so I removed my drinking privileges,*" the actor admitted.

When Jolie filed for divorce, Pitt entered Alcoholics Anonymous for a year and a half with a group of men he had not known before. This group of men brought him down to earth and helped him get in touch with his recovery process.

Recovery With A.A.

His recovery group was composed entirely of men. He said, *"I had all these men sitting around being open and honest in a way I have never heard. It was this safe space where there was little judgment, and therefore, little judgment of yourself. There's great value in that."* As the Times profile mentions; surprisingly, Pitt's time in recovery was treated with respect and not sold as a story to the press by anyone who could have seen or heard the stories. He talked about himself in Alcoholics Anonymous meetings. *"It was freeing just to expose the ugly sides of yourself,"* the actor admitted.

After his year and a half in Alcoholics Anonymous, Pitt appears to be refreshed, thanks to working through some of his issues in a group setting. He had already explained that slowly, but surely, he would take a step back from appearing on a screen when he admitted that he sees acting as a *"younger man's game"* and told The New York Times that he's keen on staying behind the camera with some producing, partially because *"producing just means you don't have to get up early and put on makeup."*

Did You Miss Drinking Alcohol?

When asked if he misses drinking alcohol, he said, *"I mean, we have a winery. I enjoy wine very, very much, but I just ran it to the ground. I had to step away for a minute. And truthfully, I could drink a Russian under the table with his vodka. I was a professional. I was good."*

He added, *"Don't want to live that way anymore,"* and said he replaced alcohol with *"cranberry juice and fizzy water,"* Happily, he said, *"I've got the cleanest urinary tract in all of LA; I guarantee you!"*

LESSONS FROM BRAD PITT'S LIFESTYLE

A sober lifestyle can be attained by anyone no matter how big of a party animal you were. It just takes determination, willpower, and a supportive group to help you stay on track, like Alcoholics Anonymous. Plus, it doesn't hurt to have six kids as an additional motivation. Ha-ha!

1. Cheers to Brad Pitt for being an inspiration to sober celebrities and party animals everywhere!

When you have hit rock bottom, the only way to go is up. For Brad Pitt, he found his saving grace in Alcoholics Anonymous and has been sober ever since. The actor has been vocal about his journey to recovery, even admitting that he was a "professional" drinker. But now, he is happier and more content than ever before.

If there's one thing we can learn from Brad Pitt, it's that it's never too late to turn your life around. The dude was 56 when he got sober, and now, he's living proof that age is just a number. No matter how old you are, it's never too late to make a change in your life. So, if you're struggling with addiction, know that it's never too late to get help. There is always light at the end of the tunnel!

2. Just because you're famous doesn't mean you're immune to addiction.

Brad Pitt is just one of many celebrities who have battled addiction. And his story is a reminder that no one is exempt from the disease of addiction. Addiction does not discriminate, no matter how rich or famous you are. If you're struggling with addiction, don't hesitate to reach out for help. There are people who care and want to see you succeed in your recovery journey.

I believe one of the reasons why Brad Pitt was able to overcome his addiction is because he had a great support system. He went to Alcoholics Anonymous meetings and had people in his life who believed in him and wanted to see him succeed. The dude even credits his six kids as one of his motivations for staying sober. If you're struggling with addiction, know that you are not alone. There are people who care about you and want to help you recover. Seek out a support group or therapy to help you in your journey to sobriety.

3. Expect setbacks but don't give up.

Recovery is not a linear process, and there will be setbacks. Brad Pitt is proof of that. He relapsed shortly after getting sober, but he didn't give up. He picked himself back up and continued his journey to recovery. If you relapse, don't beat yourself up about it. Just get back on the wagon and try again. Remember, recovery is a journey, not a destination. There will be ups and downs, but as long as you don't give up, you will eventually get to where you want to be.

4. Sobriety is possible no matter how big of a party animal you were.

Bro! Even animals can go sober. Ha-ha! Just teach a dog a new trick.

Now, I'm not saying that Brad Pitt is an animal, but he did party pretty hard in his day. And if he can sober up, anyone can! Have you ever seen the movie *Limitless*? It's about a dude who takes a pill and becomes superhuman essentially. He can do things he never could before, and his life was transformed. That's what sobriety can do for you too. It can help you tap into a side of yourself that you never knew existed. A part of you that is strong, capable, and sober. A completely new and transformed version of yourself. I mean, who doesn't want that?

5. Cranberry juice and fizzy water did it for Brad!

Yup, you read that right. When asked what his go-to drink is now that he's sober, Brad Pitt replied *"cranberry juice and fizzy water."* I'm not sure about you, but I'm definitely going to start stocking up on cranberry juice. Ha-ha! But in all seriousness, sobriety is a journey, and everyone's experience is different. Find what works for you and stick with it. Whether it's cranberry juice or something else, find your sobriety "recipe" and stick to it.

For me, it was a keto diet, working out, and NO alcohol. That was my recipe for success, and it worked like a charm! By charm, I mean I was able to stay sober for years now. But again, everyone's experience is different. Find what works for you and stick with it.

D.U.I. STORIES OF CURTIS JACKSON (50 CENT)

Curtis James Jackson, professionally known as 50 Cent, was born July 6, 1975. He is an American rapper, actor, and businessman. Known for his impact on the hip-hop industry, he has been described as a "master of the nuanced art of lyrical brevity."

Born in the South Jamaican neighborhood of Queens, Jackson began selling drugs at age 12 during the 1980s crack epidemic. He later began pursuing a musical career and produced *Power of the Dollar for Columbia Records*; however, days before the planned release, he was shot, and the album was never released.

In 2002, after 50 Cent released the mixtape *Guess Who's Back?*, he was discovered by Eminem and signed to *Shady Records* under the aegis of Dr. Dre's *Aftermath Entertainment and Interscope Records*. With the aid of Eminem and Dr. Dre, who produced his first major-label album, *Get Rich or Die Tryin*, 50 Cent became one of the world's best-selling rappers and rose to prominence as the de facto leader of East Coast hip-hop group G-Unit.

And since then, 50 Cent has become so successful in the hip-hop industry that he founded *G-Unit Records* and signed his G-Unit associates, Young Buck, Lloyd Banks, and Tony Yayo. He executive-produced, starred in a particular television series, and was slated to produce its spin-offs.

But at a particular time in his life, the hip-hop superstar 50 Cent became scared of drinking alcohol for life after becoming "paranoid" during one bad experience.

What Experience?

He told CNN host Piers Morgan, *"One incident prompted me to abstain from drinking for good. I got a chance to watch many of my mother's sisters and brothers at different periods experiment with the use of drugs or alcohol, and I see them respond so differently that I stay away. I have had an experience with alcohol that made me paranoid because of it, and I stayed away from it following that."*

During his Tycoon Pool Party in New Jersey, he was offered 50 of West Coast OG from a hit on his joint. At first, he turned it down, suggesting that the alcohol would make him pass out. But he eventually gave into peer pressure and was seen on camera getting high off its supply. 50 Cent even joked that *Tha Doggfather* got him hooked on drugs; he made him smoke weed and took alcohol that night. He captioned his Instagram video and said, *"Damn, now I have a drug problem."*

Even though he was a former drug dealer, 50 Cent has refrained from drugs and alcohol in the past. *"I don't use drugs,"* he told Piers Morgan during a 2011 interview. *"It was an easy option. You can either take $10 or $5 spent on buying weed to smoke it or put it in your pocket. When I'm out and there is nightlife, I drink. And with the way the mixologist creates different drinks with it, I am attracted to it."*

50 Cent Became Sober and Rejected His Own Champagne.

In his new book, *Hustle Harder, Hustle Smarter*, 50 Cent opened up about the challenges of remaining sober while being invested in the liquor business with his *Branson Cognac and Le Chemin Du Roi* champagne. But he figured out a way to stay social when going to the club with friends.

50 Cent is a troll, even when drinking his liquor. The Power frontman lives a sober life, no drinking or smoking. However, when it is time to be social and plug his champagne line, he's found the perfect solution to keep the party going while quietly trolling his attendees.

While promoting his new book *Hustle Harder, Hustle Smarter*, he talks about how he avoids drinking his *Branson Cognac and Le Chemin Du Roi* champagne while pushing them at parties. Instead of champagne in his cup, 50 Cent began to swap it out for something lighter.

Since he had a dilemma at the recent party in New York when Snoop Dogg offered him a joint, *"Everyone around us started cheering for me to hit it. Not wanting to kill the mood, I took a big hit and let the smoke swirl around in my mouth before I blew it back out. And that was as far as I could go."*

"For the rest of the night, I'll have that bottle in my hand," he added. *"I'll take swigs just to keep the vibe right, but I'm not drinking anything but Canada Dry. While first, I will pour drinks from a bottle of champagne for everyone in VIP with me to make sure that all my guests get drinking until the bottle is empty.*

When the bottle is empty, I will give it to one of my guys and have him quietly refill it with ginger ale and bring it back to me. For the rest of the night, I will have that bottle in my hand, parading around the new bottle taking sips here and there but not having to drink liquor. I will take swigs just to keep the vibe right, but I'm not drinking anything but Canada Dry." This was how he remained sober despite producing his own champagne. 50 Cent had a similar method when he was trying to avoid smoke.

LESSONS FROM 50 CENT'S LIFESTYLE

1. You can still have fun while staying sober by finding creative ways to enjoy yourself.

50 Cent knows how to have a good time, whether

he's at a club or hosting his own pool party. But he also knows how to stay sober, by drinking ginger ale instead of champagne or smoking tobacco instead of weed. A big part of having fun while staying sober is being creative and finding ways to enjoy yourself that don't involve drugs or alcohol. When you're sober, you may have to think outside the box a bit, but it's definitely possible to have a good time without getting drunk or high.

50 Cent understood that it's important to stay true to yourself and your sobriety goals. In order to stay sober, he didn't drink his own champagne or smoke weed, even when it would be easy to do so. He knew that if he wanted to stay sober, he must make some sacrifices and put his sobriety first. This is a great lesson for anyone who is trying to stay sober.

2. It's okay to be the odd one out.

50 Cent is usually the only sober person at the parties he goes to. But he doesn't let that stop him from having a good time. In fact, he often uses it as an opportunity to troll his friends by drinking

ginger ale instead of champagne. He knew that he was different from most people at the party, but he didn't let that stop him from enjoying himself. This is a great lesson for anyone who feels like they don't fit in because they're sober. Just because you're not drinking or doing drugs doesn't mean you can't have a good time.

3. Sometimes, you need to take a step back from your career to focus on your sobriety.

50 Cent took a break from music in order to focus on his sobriety, and it paid off. He was able to stay sober and even wrote a book about it. He knew that sometimes, you have to put your sobriety first, even if it means taking a break from your career. This is a great lesson for anyone who is struggling with addiction. Sometimes, you need to take a step back from your work or school in order to focus on your recovery. Although this may not be true for every dude out there, it is for 50 Cent, and his story can serve as an inspiration for those who are struggling with addiction.

4. You can still be successful even if you're sober.

50 Cent was offered drugs and alcohol at a party, but he didn't give in to the pressure to use them. He knew that it was important to stay sober in order to be successful. This is a great lesson for anyone who is trying to stay sober. You can still be successful even if you're not using drugs or alcohol. Just because you're sober doesn't mean you have to give up on your dreams.

CHAPTER 8

STORIES OF SOME CELEBRITIES AND HOW THEY BECAME SOBER {II}

DENZEL WASHINGTON

Denzel Washington, born in Mount Vernon, New York, on December 28, 1954, is an American actor celebrated for engaging and powerful performances. Throughout his career, he was regularly praised by critics, and his consistent success at the box office helped to dispel the perception that African American actors could not draw mainstream white audiences.

After graduating from Fordham University (B.A., 1977), Washington began to pursue acting as a career and joined the American Conservatory Theater in San Francisco. After several successful stage performances in California and New York, he made his screen debut in the comedy *Carbon Copy* (1981).

He first received national attention for his work in the drama *St. Elsewhere* (1982–88). For the film, *Cry Freedom* (1987), he portrayed South African activist Stephen Biko and received an Academy Award nomination for best supporting actor. Two years later, he won the Oscar for best supporting actor for his performance as a freed slave fighting in the Union army in the American Civil War film, *Glory* (1989).

In a cover story, the charismatic and elusive Oscar winner Denzel Washington, who played a troubled pilot in *Flight*, opened up about avoiding Hollywood hotshots, giving up alcohol for his role, and encountering an angel as a child.

In his early 30s, Denzel Washington decided to give up alcohol, which was intriguing, given that he played a pilot whose alcoholism was connected to a heart-stopping crash in his new movie, *Flight*. *"I committed to completely cut out drinking and anything that might hamper me from getting my mind and body together,"* he said. *"And the floodgates of goodness have opened upon me, spiritually and financially."*

How Did Denzel Get Sober From the Influence Of the Movie "Flight"?

Although Denzel is not so much literate, he was still someone who studies the Bible daily and said he has just been pondering Psalm 56, with its plea: *"Be merciful unto me, O God: for man would swallow me up; the fighting daily oppresseth me."* To escape certain times of his addiction, he heads out to the sea. He does not own a boat but prefers to rent one as he says that the ocean gives him a sense of peace.

Denzel stated that *Flight* came to his attention

through his late agent, Ed Limato, a man he calls "The closest thing to a father figure I had after my father passed." The last two screenplays he brought him were *Safe House* and *Flight*. One was very commercial, and the other was very dramatic. He read them and agreed to the dramatic, not knowing that would be the answer to his prayers.

Zemeckis, the writer and director, officially boarded the movie project in the spring of 2011 and made some changes to the screenplay, which Washington said was nearly in place, in contrast to *Safe House*, where he played a sociopathic CIA agent gone rogue. He was switched to act in *Flight* which opens on November 2. He said *Flight* was also in better shape, to begin with.

Many actors in Hollywood had to portray a drunk individual, including Denzel Washington, who famously took on the role of Whip Whitaker in *Flight*, the story of a pilot who miraculously crash-lands his plane after it suffers an in-flight mechanical failure while having some drinks in him.

To prepare, Washington immersed himself in technical flight manuals. Also, it spent about 20 to 30 hours using a Missile Defense Agency flight simulator in Atlanta, where the movie was shot in late 2011.

Zemeckis said he was impressed by Washington's (the actor) very detailed preparation, not just technically, but that he even asked for his props weeks ahead of time so he could walk around with a cane and get a feel for it. He said, *"As an actor, Washington is completely devoid of vanity; he brings truth to his performance alongside real gravitas and realism."*

"Curiously, I was known for the willingness to immerse myself in a role spent relatively little time talking to alcoholics. I wasn't playing an alcoholic," he argued. *"I am playing a guy who drinks; people call him an alcoholic, but he was in denial, but isn't he still an alcoholic?"* Washington paused. *"That's the title they give him,"* he conceded.

He also gave an instance of how a drunk behaves: *"One poor guy, I do not know if he was on alcohol or a stronger drug, all I could see was he's trying to do is put his slipper on for about five minutes. It taught me as much as I could have learned from anybody because watching someone in the middle of it is watching his behavior."* He leaned forward and acted a dead-on imitation of a drunk man struggling to place his tumbler on a table.

"To prepare for my role as an alcoholic pilot in the movie, I just drank every day, and I was drunk every day of shooting."

Washington, who had to play a drunk in the movie, said, *"Moderation is the key. If you drink too much water, you will drown. I am not drinking alcohol. When you are toasted (drunk), you need a day to recover. You get a hangover. So that's two days out of your life. I don't have time to waste. If there are 365 days in a year in 10 years, that's 3650, so how many days do I want to waste?"*

Acting like you are drunk when you are not drunk is more challenging than you think. When it comes to playing it, you don't play drunk but try to act sober. People don't act drunk; people are drunk, and they try to work straight. Regardless, Denzel credits a specific star for helping him get in touch with his inner drunkard, Ian McKellen.

Washington said he stopped drinking throughout the 45-day shoot, as he did on other films, including Malcolm X. *"We've all tied one on,"* he acknowledged. *"But if I had been drinking while I was shooting, it'd be harder to stay disciplined, to get up in the morning. You are a little more hungover, grouchier. I knew this was an excellent opportunity and a perfect story. So, it was something I wanted to do right, so I decided to stay sober."* Still, Washington was quick to note that his teetotaling policy was not permanent. *"But I have not given it up forever,"* he said.

DAVID HASSELHOFF

Since his starring role in "Baywatch," David Hasselhoff has become notorious for his alcoholism. His visitation rights with his daughters were temporarily suspended, forcing him to seek serious help for his addiction. A home video of a drunken Hasselhoff went viral in 2007, receiving airtime on countless news programs and across the internet.

In 2015, he told the Mirror, *"It is my responsibility to do the best I can and to take it one day at a time. But alcohol can become deadly. The scariest is when you go into a meeting, and you're like, 'Where's Steve?' And they say, 'Oh, Steve died last night. But you just met him yesterday! It's a terrifying, deadly thing that needs to be addressed."*

Indeed, Hasselhoff has taken his battles with alcohol much more seriously these days and has also decided to transform his lifestyle entirely with diet and exercise.

BRADLEY COOPER

Bradley Cooper is known for his comedic film roles. But like most of us, Cooper's life has had its ups and downs. He is recovering from alcoholism and has been sober for over a decade.

Cooper's statements attest to the fact that alcohol affects more than just yourself; it also affects those around you. In 2015, he described how alcohol affected virtually everything in his life, *"I wouldn't have been able to have access to myself or other people, or even been able to take in other people if I hadn't changed my life. I would never have been able to have the relationships that I do. I would never have been able to care for my father the way I did when he was sick. So many things."*

DANIEL RADCLIFFE

The beloved star of the "Harry Potter" movies has struggled, like many other child actors, growing up in show business. While his character Harry was innocent and heroic, for Daniel Radcliffe, real-life challenges started affecting him, namely his addiction to alcohol.

In a 2012 interview published in Shortlist magazine, Radcliffe stated how he realized that *"drinking was unhealthy and damaging to my body and my social life"* and how he had become *"a recluse at 20."* He even admitted how he used to drink before going on the set and confided in co-star Gary Oldman who'd also be addicted to alcohol.

Despite being sober, Radcliffe admits it's not easy to maintain sobriety at events where there's alcohol. One of his greatest lessons is that he had to want a sober life for himself. He stated in the same interview, *"I had to stop myself. And stopping has shown me a world of happiness that I didn't think was possible."* This is a lesson that we can all learn from Radcliffe.

CARRIE FISHER

Aside from her fame as Princess Leia in "Star Wars," Carrie Fisher was also well-known for her public statements about her health and addictions. This included alcohol. In 2008, she even published a book about her struggles called "Wishful Drinking."

In the book, she wrote, *"Happiness is one of the many things I'm likely to experience for a day and certainly throughout a lifetime. But I think if you expect that you're going to be happy throughout your life, more to the point if you need to be comfortable all the time; well, among other things, you have the makings of a classic drug addict or alcoholic."* Indeed, alcohol is often used as a coping mechanism, and Fisher described in her usual humorous fashion how drinking can worsen this.

Tragically, Fisher died of a heart attack in December 2016. Fans continue to mourn the loss of the endearing actress. It is thought that relapse was partially to blame.

STEPHEN KING

World-famous horror novelist Stephen King struggled with drugs and alcohol for a considerable period. In 1987, King's family and friends staged an intervention, dumping evidence of his addictions in front of him. King immediately sought help and quit all drugs and alcohol in the late 1980s.

In 2013, King opened up to The Guardian about his former alcohol addiction, describing how he's not ashamed of his past. He said, *"There's a thing in A.A., something they read in many meetings, 'The Promises.' Most of those promises have come true in my life. We'll come to know a new freedom and happiness; that's true. But it also says, 'We will not regret the past nor wish to shut the door on it.' And I have no wish to shut the door in the past. I have been pretty upfront about my past. But do I regret it? I do. I do. I regret the necessity."*

King's not about to pretend he didn't have struggles with alcohol nor does he think he should hide it. It's a part of who he is, and he's been sober since his family intervention.

MAJOR LESSONS FROM STEPHEN KING'S LIFESTYLE

1. Don't be ashamed of your past

King is refreshingly open about his struggles with addiction, and he doesn't try to hide them. He recognized that it was a part of who he is, but he didn't let it define him. Allowing yourself to be open about your past can help you move on from it and prevent you from making the same mistakes again. With addiction, honesty is always the best policy.

2. Seek help when you need it

King's family staged an intervention when they saw how addiction was starting to take over his life. He immediately sought professional help and has been sober ever since. This shows that it's never too late to get help for addiction. No matter how bad things seem, there is always hope for recovery.

Life is always better when you have the support of others. In his interview with The Guardian, King mentions how important it is to have people in your life who care about you and want to help you through tough times. If you're struggling with addiction, reach out to your loved ones and let them know what's going on. They can be a great source of support and strength.

3. Sobriety can bring new happiness and freedom

King said that many of the promises made in Alcoholics Anonymous have come true for him. One of those promises is that "sober individuals will experience new happiness and freedom." This is something that many people in recovery can attest to. When you're no longer controlled by addiction, you're free to live your life the way you want to. You may be surprised at how much joy and happiness sobriety can bring.

King said, *"There's a thing in A.A., something they read in a lot of meetings, The Promises. Most of those promises have come true in my life: we'll come to know a new freedom and new happiness, that's true. But it also says in there: we will not regret the past nor wish to shut the door on it."*

Guys, the above King's statement is so powerful. It's one thing to come to terms with your past and accept it, but it's another thing entirely to be able to look back on it without any regrets. That's what recovery is all about. Once you're in recovery, you can start living your life to the fullest and enjoy all the wonderful things that sobriety has to offer.

ROBIN WILLIAMS

The famous comedian abused cocaine and alcohol early in his career but quit when a friend and fellow comedian, John Belushi, died of a cocaine and heroin overdose in 1982. After that, the late actor struggled off and on with alcohol for years until his death in 2014. He even regularly highlighted these struggles as a part of his stand-up routines.

In a 2006 interview with Diane Sawyer, Williams talked about the reality that drinking doesn't always have a reason behind it. *"It's [addiction], not caused by anything; it's just there,"* Williams said.

"It waits. It lays in wait for when you think, 'It's fine now, I'm OK.' Then, the next thing you know, it's not OK. Then you realize, 'Where am I?' I didn't realize I was in Cleveland." Sadly, Williams died in 2014. He was reported to have just entered rehab again shortly before his death.

LESSONS FROM ROBIN WILLIAMS' LIFESTYLE

1. Addiction can happen to anyone

No matter how successful or famous you are, addiction can still take over your life. Williams was a hugely successful actor and comedian, but that didn't stop him from struggling with addiction. This just goes to show that addiction doesn't discriminate. It can affect anyone, no matter who they are. The important thing is to get help if you're struggling.

3. Relapse is always a possibility

Williams struggled with addiction for many years and had several relapses. This just goes to show that relapse is always a possibility, no matter how long you've been sober. If you're in recovery, it's important to be mindful of this and to always stay on the lookout for signs that you might be slipping. If you do start to struggle, reach out for help right away.

Despite his struggles, Williams was able to achieve sobriety several times throughout his life. This just goes to show that recovery is possible, no matter how many times you relapse. If you're struggling with addiction, don't give up. There is hope and help available.

BETTY FORD

Betty Ford, the wife of former President Gerald Ford, suffered from alcoholism and addiction to painkillers. She raised public awareness of addiction by confessing her long-time battle with alcoholism in the 1970s. When she finally recovered, she established the Betty Ford Center to help others overcome substance and alcohol abuse.

Perhaps Ford's most incredible legacy was the honesty she brought to the American idea of alcoholism. Alcohol addiction can happen to anyone. She said, *"My makeup wasn't smeared. I wasn't disheveled. I behaved politely, and I never finished off a bottle, so how could I be an alcoholic?"* In other words, there are no stereotypical symptoms of alcoholism. Even being the first lady of the United States doesn't make you immune to alcoholism.

UNIQUE LESSONS FROM BETTY FORD'S LIFESTYLE

1. Alcoholism doesn't have a "type"

As Ford points out, there is no one type of person who suffers from alcoholism. It can affect anyone, no matter who they are or what they do. This is why it's so important to be aware of the signs and symptoms of addiction. If you think you might be struggling, don't be afraid to reach out for help.

2. Treatment is important

Ford sought treatment for her addiction and eventually recovered. This just goes to show that treatment can be incredibly effective in helping people overcome addiction. If you're struggling with addiction, don't be afraid to seek help from a professional. With treatment, you can overcome your addiction and start living a sober, healthy life. Ford's story is another proof that sobriety is possible, no matter how long you've been struggling with addiction. If you're ready to make a change, there is help available. You can overcome your addiction and start living a healthy, sober life.

MEL GIBSON

Mel Gibson has publicly admitted to battling alcoholism all his adult life. He was arrested in 2009 for driving under the influence. In a previous 2006 arrest based on suspected drunk driving, the arresting officer claimed he made anti-Semitic remarks. In the past, Gibson sought professional help and checked himself into rehab for his alcohol problem.

In 2016, The Fix reported Gibson laying out the harsh reality that comes with thinking about quitting alcohol. *"They say there are only three options: You go insane, die, or quit."*

Even with this bleak outlook, Gibson remains sober today and is an outspoken critic of alcoholism.

Gibson's experience with addiction can teach us a lot about the disease.

IMPORTANT LESSONS FROM MEL GIBSON'S LIFESTYLE

1. You rather face death than keep living with addiction

For some people, the thought of quitting alcohol is so daunting that they would rather keep drinking and risk death. This was Gibson's thinking before he finally got sober. If you're struggling with addiction, it's important to realize that you don't have to keep suffering. There is help available, and sobriety is possible. Death doesn't have to be the result of addiction.

2. **Alcoholism is a lifelong battle**

Gibson has been battling alcoholism for his entire adult life. This just goes to show that addiction is a chronic, relapsing disease. If you're struggling with addiction, it's important to seek help from a professional. With treatment, you can learn how to manage your addiction and live a sober, healthy life.

3. Rehab can be effective

Although Gibson has relapsed in the past, he has

also sought professional help for his addiction. He even checked himself into rehab at one point. This just goes to show that treatment can be effective in helping people overcome addiction. If you're struggling with addiction, don't be afraid to seek help from a professional. With treatment, you can overcome your addiction and start living a sober, healthy life.

4. Addiction can lead to serious consequences

Gibson's arrest for drunk driving led to some serious consequences, including the loss of several acting gigs. This just goes to show that addiction can have a major impact on your life. Imagine if he would have chosen to get help before his arrest. He may have been able to avoid these negative consequences altogether.

LINDSAY LOHAN

The young starlet, like many child actresses, has publicly struggled with drug and alcohol abuse. Lohan has to work hard to stay sober and has already had one failed attempt at rehab in 2011.

Lohan has also been honest about other dangers

alcohol can pose. In 2010, she was forced by a court order to wear an alcohol detection bracelet to monitor her alcohol consumption. In 2014, Lohan had a public relapse on her reality show, demonstrating how beating alcohol addiction is an ongoing battle. In a 2013 interview with Oprah Winfrey, Lohan said that alcohol *"was a gateway to other things for me. I tried cocaine with alcohol."*

These celebrities illustrate that alcohol is often used to self-medicate—to alleviate life's stressors. Their honesty about their struggles is both heartbreaking and endearing. ***There is a lot more inspiration from celebrities who have publicly talked about these struggles. When alcohol consumption becomes abusive, it's time to seek treatment. It's essential to address the underlying issues to treat alcohol addiction.*** In the next chapter, let's learn more about alcohol abuse and addiction and explore treatment options that can help avoid adverse health outcomes.

DMC

It's no secret that alcoholism can destroy lives. It takes a toll on the drinker's health, wrecks relationships, and can ruin finances. For rapper DMC, his battle with the bottle nearly cost him everything.

This dude was the Devastating Mic Controller, but he struggled to get a handle on his own life. When the alcohol wasn't enough to fill the hole in his heart and drive away the paralyzing depression, DMC seriously considered suicide. Isn't that weird?

DMC, real name Darryl McDaniels, struggled with alcohol for years, and it took a heavy toll on his life. In a new book, "Ten Ways Not to Commit Suicide," the rap legend opened up about his battle with depression and suicidal thoughts, and how alcohol nearly killed him.

McDaniels said that he started drinking at just 13 years old, and by the time he was in his twenties, he was drinking a case of beer every day. Isn't that insane? He was guzzling so much alcohol that he almost destroyed his liver and pancreas.

His drinking led to health problems, and he was eventually warned by a doctor that if he didn't stop, he would die.

So, he quit drinking for nearly a decade, but the depression set in. And without alcohol to numb the pain, his suicidal thoughts became more frequent. McDaniels said that his vocal problems were a big part of his downfall. He struggled with a condition called spasmodic dysphonia, which caused involuntary movements of the voice box muscles. This made it difficult for him to rap, and he felt embarrassed and rejected by his bandmates. That's what happens when you can't get your life together; your friends start to abandon you.

Fortunately, McDaniels was able to get help and turn his life around. He's been sober for years now, and he's using his story to help others who are struggling.

From all indications, it's clear that alcoholism is a serious problem, and it can have a devastating impact on every aspect of a person's life. For DMC, it nearly cost him everything. The dude has been sober **since 2004**. But even after he got clean, his wife said he still wasn't back to 100 percent. *"He came back, and to me, he wasn't still himself,"* said Zuri. This goes to show that addiction can have a lasting impact, even after someone gets sober.

BARACK OBAMA'S FATHER

Barack Obama's father was a straight-up alcoholic. The dude caused all kinds of problems for his family, including Obama's mother. It's no wonder the formal president has been tight-lipped about his father's struggles with addiction; it's a painful reminder of the damage alcohol can cause.

Obama Sr. wasn't just any alcoholic; he was a serious abuser. He would beat his wives, including Obama's mother, and he was notoriously absent during his son's childhood. The pain and suffering that Obama's father caused is a powerful reminder of why sobriety is the best lifestyle choice.

Although Obama did not grow up with his father, he acknowledged the pain that his father's alcoholism caused. In a 2009 interview with

CNN, Obama said: *"It's no secret that my father was a troubled person. Anybody who has read my first book, 'Dreams from My Father,' knows that, you know, he had an alcoholism problem, and that he didn't treat his families very well."*

It is clear that Obama's father had a profound impact on his life, even though they were not close. The trauma of growing up with an alcoholic parent can stay with a person for their entire life. Thankfully, Obama has chosen to live a sober lifestyle and is an advocate for responsible drinking. He is living proof that it is possible to overcome the damage caused by alcoholism.

His half-brother, Mark Ndesandjo, has also written a book about their father's alcoholism and its effects on the family. In an interview with CNN, Ndesandjo said: *"I felt that my brother—at that time—felt that I was too white. And I thought he was too black."* This quote perfectly captures the tension that can exist between siblings when the family is not functioning properly.

It's clear that alcoholism has had a huge impact

on the Obama family. It's a reminder of the pain and suffering that addiction can cause, and it's a testament to the strength of the human spirit that both Barack Obama and Mark Ndesandjo have overcome their father's alcoholism to lead successful and sober lives.

Ndesandjo is the half-brother of Barack Obama. Unlike the formal president, he lived with their father for a time as a child. In his book, Ndesandjo painted a picture of a man who was consumed by alcoholism and abusive towards his family.

Ndesandjo further claimed that his father held a knife to his mother's throat and threatened to kill her. This is just one example of the abuse that Obama's father inflicted on his family.

It's clear that addiction can have a profound and lasting impact on families. The Obama family is just one example of how alcoholism can tear a family apart. Thankfully, both Barack and Mark have chosen to lead sober lives and are using their experiences to help others.

While Obama has spoken about his father's alcoholism in interviews, he has never done so in such detail. In the book, Ndesandjo described how their father would often drink to excess and become violent.

This story goes to show that alcoholism isn't hereditary, but it can be passed down through learned behaviors. However, Ndesandjo and Obama both chose to live sober lives, despite having an alcoholic father. This is clearly a matter of choice, not destiny.

CHAPTER 9

NFL PLAYERS

HENRY RUGGS

Henry Ruggs was a renowned NFL player who had it all. Henry Ruggs was a three-sport athlete in high school and played college football in Alabama. Ruggs was the fastest player in the 2020 NFL Combine and was selected by the Raiders in the first round of the 2020 NFL Draft. But his life spiraled out of control after he developed a drinking problem. Alcoholism turned Ruggs into a shell of his former self and ultimately led to him being involved in a deadly

D.U.I. crash.

Ruggs was driving more than 150 mph with a blood alcohol level twice Nevada's legal limit when he crashed his car into an SUV. The vehicle went up in flames, and the victim, along with her dog, perished in the fire. Ruggs was charged with a felony D.U.I.—resulting in death, felony, and reckless driving.

The former Alabama standout appeared in court on Wednesday 2021, where prosecutors alleged that Ruggs was driving at a speed of 156 mph just two seconds before the crash. A loaded gun was found in Rugg's car, and his blood-alcohol level was more than double the legal limit. Ruggs was released from the Raiders shortly after the incident.

It's tragic when anyone dies as a result of drunk driving, but it's especially devastating when it's someone with so much potential like Henry Ruggs. His once-promising career and life were ruined by alcoholism. This is a cautionary tale about the dangers of drinking and driving.

Folks, if you've been hitting the sauce a little too

hard lately, take Henry Ruggs' story as a warning. It's not worth it to risk your life and the lives of others by getting behind the wheel drunk. Let this be a lesson to us all. Staying sober is underrated; I mean look at Henry Ruggs, look where it got him. You don't want to end up like that.

Ruggs was held on $150,000 bail and is required to wear electronic monitoring if he's released. You can bet that his once-bright future is now permanently dimmed. Alcoholism is a serious disease that can ruin lives. If you or someone you know is struggling with addiction, please get help. There are resources available to assist you on your road to recovery. Don't let alcoholism control your life like it did Henry Ruggs.

With so much potential, it's a shame to see someone like Henry Ruggs fall victim to alcoholism. It just goes to show that no one is immune to this. From the outside looking in, it may have seemed like Ruggs had everything going for him, but addiction is a powerful force. It can take down even the biggest and brightest stars. The after-effects of this crash will be felt by Ruggs and the victim's family for years to come. Let this be a reminder to folks that drinking and driving is never worth it.

For a 22-year-old man, Henry Ruggs has made some big mistakes in his short life. He's lucky to be alive after his involvement in a fatal D.U.I. crash. Ruggs had a promising future ahead of him, but that was all derailed by alcoholism. This is a cautionary tale about the dangers of alcoholism and drunk driving, and I cannot stress enough how important it is always to stay sober. One mistake can cost you everything. Just ask Henry Ruggs.

Ruggs' conviction carries a sentence of two to 20 years in prison. This is a tragedy that could have easily been avoided! The dude legit had everything going for him, but let alcoholism take over, and now, his life is ruined. 20 straight years in the penitentiary! That's a tough pill to swallow.

As someone who's struggled with alcoholism, I can attest to how powerful addiction can be. It takes over your life and controls you in ways you never thought possible. Ruggs is a tragedy all around. A young promising life was ruined and cut short by addiction. When will people learn?

LEONARD LITTLE

Back in 1998, Leonard Little killed a woman while driving drunk. He was convicted of involuntary manslaughter and spent 90 days in jail, 4 years probation, and 1,000 hours of community service. The NFL suspended him for eight games in 1999.

Guys, if there's any industry where you're supposed to learn from your mistakes, it's the NFL. That's why it's so frustrating to see a player like Leonard Little still making the same stupid mistakes, over and over again.

It's a shame because Leonard Little was a talented player. But when you keep making stupid decisions like driving drunk, you're not giving teams much of a choice but to move on without you.

It's especially sad when you consider how much pain and suffering Little has caused other people. In addition to killing the woman in 1998, he still couldn't keep his name off the police blotter.

It's a damn shame when someone with so much

talent throws it all away because he can't keep his nose clean. That's exactly what Leonard Little did, again and again.

Later, he was arrested for making some threats and harassing phone calls to his ex-girlfriend. Then, not even a year later, he got pulled over for drunk driving. But because he's a talented football player, he manages to weasel his way out of that one too.

But folks, the real kicker is that this isn't even the first time he's been arrested for drunk driving. Little failed three sobriety tests and was arrested. After he posted bond, prosecutors wanted to pursue a felony charge on him, citing his past troubles.

It's just unbelievable that someone can be so selfish and reckless. It's clear that Leonard Little has a serious problem with alcohol, and yet, he still doesn't seem to be taking any responsibility for his actions. At this point, it's hard to feel sorry for him anymore. What's even more infuriating is that, despite all his legal troubles, Leonard Little is still a very talented football player.

Folks, this is a clear indication that no matter the talent you have and no matter what you're able to accomplish on the field, if you don't have your life together off the field, it will eventually catch up to you.

It's a sorry case when alcoholism takes over somebody's life, and they just can't seem to help themselves. That was the case with Leonard Little, whose drinking led to him getting behind the wheel of a car while intoxicated, killing another human being in the process.

This isn't some sob story, either. This is a cold hard fact: Leonard Little killed someone while driving drunk, and he deserves whatever punishment he gets.

Now, I'm not saying that alcoholism is a choice. It's just like a disease, and it can take over somebody's life without them even realizing it. But that doesn't excuse what Little did. He knew damn well that getting behind the wheel of a car while drunk was wrong, and he did it anyway.

And for what? Was he trying to impress someone or show off how much he could drink? Whatever the reason, it was a stupid and selfish act that has forever changed the lives of both him and the victim's family.

The victim's son, Michael Gutweiler, has every right to be angry. In fact, I'm surprised he wasn't angrier. He's shown a lot of restraint in how he's dealt with this whole situation.

"If he thinks he's this big, celebrity hot-shot football player, go out and rent a limo when you're drinking," Gutweiler said of Little. *"You have a $7 million contract. How stupid are you? That's just common sense."*

It's tragic when somebody so young has to deal with something like this, but that's the reality of the situation. And while I can't even begin to imagine what Gutweiler went through, I do know that he handled the whole thing with a lot more grace than I ever could.

In the end, Leonard Little made a mistake that cost someone her life. There's no excuse for it, and he needs to be held accountable for his actions. Anything less would be a travesty.

Folks, this is the real world. There are consequences for your actions. And in Leonard Little's case, those consequences are well deserved. It is just too sad that an innocent victim had to pay the ultimate price for his stupidity. Alcoholism is a disease, but that doesn't make what Little did any less heinous. Hopefully, he'll get the help he needs, but even if he does, he'll have to live with what he's done for the rest of his life. 1988 may be a long time ago, but for Michael Gutweiler, it probably feels like yesterday. That's the power of grief. It never goes away; it just fades with time. And in this case, time will never heal the wound.

DONTE STALLWORTH

Donte Stallworth is a prime example of how alcohol can destroy not just one life, but many. On March 14, 2009, Stallworth hit and killed 59-year-old, Mario Reyes, while driving drunk in Miami, Florida. The impact of this tragedy was felt far and wide. Reyes was the breadwinner for his family, leaving behind a wife and a daughter who were suddenly faced with immense financial hardship. Reyes's family will never be able to forget the pain and suffering that Stallworth inflicted upon them.

But it's not just the Reyes family who has been affected by Stallworth's actions. The NFL player also pled guilty to D.U.I. manslaughter, which carries a maximum sentence of 15 years in prison. However, because of his clean record and cooperation with authorities, Stallworth only received a sentence of 30 days in jail, 10 years probation, and 1,000 hours of community service.

He was suspended by the NFL for the entire 2009 season, and his career has been forever tarnished. As a result of his actions, Stallworth has also had to live with the knowledge that he took another human being's life.

So, what can we learn from all this? A drunken lifestyle is never worth it, no matter who you are. The pain and suffering that Donte Stallworth has caused is a testament to that. If you or someone you know is struggling with alcoholism, please get help. It's not worth risking your life or the lives of others.

Donte Stallworth made a split-second decision to get behind the wheel after drinking alcohol, and that decision changed his life forever. It's a decision that has had a ripple effect on so many people, and one that Stallworth will have to live with for the rest of his life. If there's anything we can take away from this tragedy, it's that alcohol always has consequences. It's simply not worth the risk.

In other words, the dude is a straight-up killer. He hit and killed some dude while he was drunk driving, and only got 30 days in jail? That ain't shit. That guy's family will never be the same, and all because Stallworth decided to drink and drive. He's a scumbag of the highest order, and justice wasn't really served in this case. If you ask me, he got off way too easy. But the dent in his reputation will be with him forever. The dude is a straight-up murderer.

Again, being sober all your life is extremely important not just for yourself but also for others. Take it from Donte Stallworth, who killed a man while driving drunk and will forever have to live with that on his conscience. It's not worth it, homie. Just don't do it. In one of his interviews, he said: "*It was the worst decision of my life. I wish I could go back and change what happened, but I can't.*"

Trust me guys, alcohol is not worth it. It's not worth the hangovers, the blackouts, or the risk of taking someone's life. Just don't do it. Although Donte got 30, that was 2009 folks; this is 2022, and the world is a different place. You could be charged with second-degree murder and get 25 years of your life. Just think about that the next time you want to take a sip of alcohol. Your life could be changed forever. Soberness is still the best way to go!

JOSH BRENT

Josh Brent was a rising star in the NFL until he made the mistake of driving drunk and crashing his car, killing his teammate Jerry Brown Jr. in the process. Brent was sentenced to 180 days in jail and 10 years probation but could have faced up to

20 years behind bars.

Brent's mother wept as the sentence was read, but the judge had harsh words for the former Dallas Cowboys lineman. *"Your actions bring shame to the city of Dallas,"* Judge Robert Burns told Brent. *"Mr. Brent, you are not the first Dallas Cowboy to kill somebody with a vehicle, but I sure hope you are the last."*

The prosecutor in the case said that Brent is still in shock at the sentence and called it a "tragedy" for all involved.

This is a tragedy on so many levels. For Josh Brent, it was a big blow to his football career and potentially much more. For Jerry Brown Jr.'s family, it's the loss of a son and brother. And for society as a whole, it's another reminder of the dangers of drunk driving.

Having previously been convicted of D.U.I., Brent should have known better than to get behind the wheel after drinking. But he made the mistake of thinking he could handle it, and now, he'll have to live with the consequences for the rest of his life.

Sober lifestyle is the best way to avoid such a fate. This also goes to show that alcoholism can ruin even the brightest of futures. If Josh Brent had been able to stay sober, he wouldn't be convicted for the same crime, and Jerry Brown Jr. might still be alive today.

It's a hard lesson, and there are no winners here, only losers. And that's why a sober lifestyle is the best. The dude was driving at like 110 mph while drunk as shit. He killed his teammate and fucked up his own life in the process. Sober lifestyle for the win!

With the average sentence of 51 months for manslaughter, we have three NFL players who served a combined 204 days in jail.

It's time for society to wake up and realize that alcoholism is a serious problem that needs to be dealt with. Too many lives are being ruined or lost because of it. Henry Ruggs, Leonard Little, and Josh Brent are just examples of this, but there are thousands of others out there who are facing the same issue.

So, let's start by changing the way we think about alcoholism. It's not a "party-hard" thing or a sign of weakness. It's a real thing that can ruin lives if it's not dealt with properly.

Let's make something very clear. I am not using these stories of other people's drinking issues to ridicule them but to display that some of our heroes will also find themselves battling alcoholism. Because, unlike some powers present, alcoholism is not biased or racist. Your social status will not protect you when alcohol takes power over your life; in fact, your status will only worsen the situation.

One way is by becoming your enabler. When I got my first D.U.I., I received a slap on the wrist, enabling me to continue to live the same lifestyle without penalty. This is similar to the mentioned NFL players that actually caused the death of a person. No real penalty, or help, and no change.

CHAPTER 10

PROMINENT CELEBRITIES THAT LOST THEIR LIVES DUE TO DRUGS

MICHAEL JACKSON

As you all know, MJ was one of the most talented performers of our generation. I need not remind y'all of his accomplishments, because they're too many to list. What I will say is that this dude was seriously fucked up on drugs for the last 15 years of his life.

I'm not talking about the occasional joint or line of cocaine. I'm talking about heavy-duty shit like opioids and propofol—the surgical anesthetic that eventually killed him. And according to experts, his addiction was "quite extensive."

Now, I'm not here to judge MJ. Hell, we all have our vices and weaknesses. But what I am here to say is that drugs fucked up his life, and the lives of those around him.

According to testimony given in a wrongful death trial against concert promoter AEG Live, Jackson was "quite extensive" in his drug use during the last 15 years of his life.

This addiction caused great pain and suffering for both Jackson himself and those who loved him. His family had to watch him go through the motions of addiction, never knowing when he would be clean or when he would relapse. As a result, many fans were left devastated when Jackson died of an overdose in 2009.

The dude was putting himself at serious risk during the preparation for his 2009 comeback tour, and nobody knew because he was so secretive about it. It's a shame too because if people had known, maybe they could've helped him get clean before it was too late.

But addiction is a tricky thing as anyone who's struggled with it knows. It can be hard to resist the temptation to get high, especially when you're in the throes of addiction. That's why it's so important for those who are addicted to get help from professionals who can guide them through the process of recovery.

Let's all take a moment to remember MJ, but also to learn from his story. Drugs can ruin lives. Don't let them ruin yours. Stay strong and stay sober.

Although the king of pop is gone for sure, his history will live on forever. And while we all enjoy his songs, let's not forget the pain and suffering that addiction can cause. It's just not worth it in the end. Sober is still the way to go!

PRINCE

When the news of Prince's death broke on April 21, 2016, everyone was shocked. Not simply because of his untimely death, but the cause. In the public eye, Prince led a healthy life. He was a dedicated vegan, and according to his cousin Chazz Smith, he avoided drugs and alcohol his entire life: *"I can tell you this – what I know is that he was perfectly healthy."*

Prince was said to have "limitless energy" according to journalist Heather McElhatton who worked with the singer in the 1990s. *"He could shoot for two days straight, without getting tired, it seems,"* Heather stated. *"I never saw him eat, like physically eat, anything in 10 years ... never saw him drink."*

Perhaps the only Prince's indulgence known publicly was his love for coffee, particularly a chocolate cooler with no whipped cream.

But an autopsy revealed something not known by the public in the entire 41 years of his career. He was addicted, isolated, and in pain.

The drug that supposedly killed Prince was described as "legal heroin on steroids" by the experts. Although fentanyl is legally manufactured and distributed in America, it is said to be 30 times stronger than heroin.

Throughout the 41 years of high-voltage performance, sometimes jumping on stage in heels and not a single sign of breaking down, someone should have guessed that Prince was hiding something. Unfortunately, his addiction and intervention came too late.

WHITNEY HOUSTON

Here is another cautionary tale of the dangers of drugs, this time starring Whitney Houston. The late singer's life was plagued by drug addiction, and it eventually led to her untimely death.

Whitney Houston is one of the most successful singers of all time. She has sold over 200 million records and has won numerous awards, including five Grammy Awards. However, her life was not always glamorous. I mean, sure, she had a successful career and all, but her personal life was a mess.

Houston struggled with drug addiction for many years. In 2002, she admitted to using cocaine, alcohol, crack, and marijuana in an interview with Diane Sawyer. Houston's addiction took a toll on her personal life and her career. She divorced Bobby Brown in 2007, and her career stalled in recent years.

Sadly, Houston's addiction led to her death. In 2012, she was found dead in a hotel room bathtub. An autopsy later revealed that she had cocaine in her system.

Toxicology results also showed Houston had marijuana, Xanax, Flexeril, and Benadryl in her body. I mean, she really liked her drugs. But that's not all… Further investigations show that due to years of drug and alcohol abuse, the "Bodyguard" star was left with a damaged heart and liver, a hole in her nose, and 11 front teeth missing. Guys, this is freaking sad. I can see how deeply addiction can ruin someone's life.

Her daughter, Bobbi Kristina Brown, was hospitalized after she was found unresponsive in a bathtub just three years later. Thankfully, she survived but died six months later due to a drug-related lifestyle. We cannot rule out the fact that the trauma of losing her mother clearly took a toll on her. This just goes to show that addiction can destroy families, not just individuals.

It's tragic when anyone dies from drug addiction, but it's especially sad when it's someone as talented as Whitney Houston. The details of Houston's death are a sobering reminder of the dangers of drug addiction. I mean, sure, we all like to party every now and then. But when drugs start to take over your life, it's time to get help. There's nothing cool about drug addiction. It ruins lives and destroys families, and it will continue to do so until we as a society learn to stay sober a.f.!

For fact, staying sober is the best way to live. You are in control of your own life, and you don't have to worry about ending up like Whitney Houston. So, yeah. Drugs are bad, okay? If you're struggling with addiction, please get help. And if you're not addicted to drugs, don't start using them. Just say no, kids. Whitney Houston is a perfect example of why drugs are bad news.

BOBBY BROWN'S CHILDREN

When you think of Bobby Brown, you think of a bad boy who just couldn't stay out of trouble. From his days as a member of New Edition to his tumultuous marriage to the late Whitney Houston, Bobby Brown was always making headlines, and not always for the right reasons.

But what many people don't know is that Bobby Brown's problems with drugs and alcohol started long before he ever became famous. His parents were both alcoholics, and Bobby began drinking and using drugs at a very young age.

Bobby's addiction problems quickly spiraled out of control, and he began to behave erratically both on and off stage. He was arrested multiple times for drug possession and D.U.I., and he even served time in jail. I mean, the dude even crashed his car while high on cocaine!

Needless to say, Bobby's drug use took a toll on his health, his relationships, and his career. Following the death of Houston on February 11, 2012, six days after his 43rd birthday, Brown struggled to perform at a New Edition show, shouting *"I love you, Whitney"* in tears. Brown then excused himself from the stage, and New Edition finished the remainder of the show without him.

In November 2020, his son, Bobby Brown Jr., was found dead at the age of 28 from an apparent drug overdose of alcohol, cocaine, and the powerful opioid fentanyl, according to a coroner's report. This was just two months prior, Bobbi Kristina— Bobby's only child with Whitney Houston—died from an overdose at the age of 22.

Bobbi Kristina died from complications due to drug use in 2015—just three years after Whitney Houston's (her mother's) death. Bobbi Kristina was found face down and unresponsive in a bathtub, reportedly after using drugs. She later died, and Bobby was devastated.

Bobby has said that he believes his daughter's

death was "God's way of telling me to stop."

It's clear that drugs have taken a huge toll on Bobby Brown's life. He's lost friends, family members, and even his career because of his addiction. Thankfully, he's now sober and is using his story to help others who are struggling with addiction.

Since then, Bobby has been on a mission to turn his life around. He's been sober for several years now, and he's working hard to help others who are struggling with addiction.

Bobby Brown's story is a cautionary tale about the dangers of drug addiction. His struggles have caused pain and heartache for his family, friends, and fans. His lifestyle influenced and killed his children and wife; it's a miracle he's still alive himself. The dude's been through a lot, and we hope he continues to stay sober and help others who are struggling with addiction. It's clear that Bobby Brown is proof that a sober life is the best lifestyle.

DMX

Throughout his career, late rapper Earl Simmons, popularly known by the stage name DMX, was always open about his struggles with substance addiction, which started when he was 14 after he was pressured into smoking crack cocaine. Reflecting on the incident that changed his life forever, the rapper explained in November 2020:

"I didn't smoke cigarettes. I didn't smoke weed. I didn't do anything at 14 years old... He passed the blunt around and... I hit the blunt. I never felt like this before; it f-ed me up. I later found that he laced the blunt with a crack. Why would you do that to a child? He was like 30, and he knew I looked up to him. Why would you do that to somebody who looks up to you?"

Soon after this episode, Simmons's career took off, but unfortunately, so did his drug usage. He had plenty of run-ins with the law and entered rehabs several times, even sometimes canceling concerts. His former schoolmate, friend, and fellow New York rapper Jay Z tried many times to rescue DMX, even donating $1 million to get him to special rehab and signing him to his own music label *Roc Nation*. DMX battled with drug addiction throughout his life whilst releasing a string of number-one albums. Unfortunately, he died at 50 on April 9, 2021, of a drug overdose.

MAC MILLER

Miller joins the list of young, promising rappers who have died due to drug overdoses.

Mac Miller was an American rapper who sadly died of an accidental drug overdose in 2018. He was only 26 years old. I mean dude was seriously talented. He had just won a Grammy award nomination for his album *Swimming*, which was released posthumously. But despite all his success, Mac Miller was no stranger to demons and addiction.

In fact, he often rapped about his struggles with substance abuse in his music. On the Faces mixtape, he even opened up with the line *"shoulda*

died already (faces). Came in, I was high already."
And in a recent interview with Vulture, he spoke
about the pressure of being young and making
mistakes in the public eye.

*"A lot of times in my life, I've put this pressure to
hold myself to the standard of whatever I thought
I was supposed to be or how I was supposed to
be perceived… It's annoying to be out and have
someone come up to me and think they know.
They're like 'Yo, man, are you okay?' I'm like 'Yeah,
I'm fuckin at the grocery store.' You know?"* Miller
said.

It's just so sad that someone with so much talent
and potential could be taken away so soon. And
it's even sadder when you realize that it was all
because of drugs. It just goes to show you that
addiction doesn't discriminate. It doesn't matter
how much money you have, how successful you
are, or how young or old you are. Addiction will
fuck you up.

Hommies, if you're reading this and you're
struggling with addiction, please get help. It's

not worth losing your life over. Trust me, I know from experience. Do you really want your parents to have to bury you? Your friends? Your fans? I didn't think so. You either wait for addiction to kill you, or you kill it first. The choice is yours. But I hope you choose life. Sobriety is the best way to go. It's not always easy, but it's worth it. I promise.

Stories like these always remind me of how precious life is and how we need to cherish every moment. You never know when it's going to be your time to go. So, make the most of it while you can. Live your life to the fullest and don't let anything hold you back. However, please don't make the same mistakes that Mac Miller did. Drugs will only lead you down a dark path. Trust me, I know from experience. So, stay away from that shit and live your best life. That's all I can say.

JUICE WRLD

The late Juice WRLD was a highly successful and popular rap artist. However, his life was cut short due to a drug overdose at the age of 21. Drugs had a profound and negative impact on Juice WRLD's life, causing him immense pain and suffering, as well as heartbreak for his fans and family.

Juice WRLD was a heavy drug user during his childhood and teens. He began drinking Lean and using Percocet and Xanax in his sixth grade. I mean this dude was using some hardcore drugs at a young age. This isn't something to be taken lightly. It's scary a.f.

As his fame and fortune grew, so did his drug use. He continued to abuse Lean and Percocet, as well as taking other drugs. These drugs took a toll on Juice WRLD's health, causing him to have seizures and suffer from anxiety and depression.

In one song, he even raps about how he would take pills over and over again. He also talks about how his girlfriend hates it when he gets too high, but that's where he feels he belongs. It's clear that Juice WRLD was in a very dark place due to his drug addiction.

"F–k one dose, I need two pills, two pills. I'm lookin' for trouble so I know I'm gonna find it. Ring, ring, plug hit my phone, perfect timin'. I know I'm not

right. But I'm not wrong, no, I'm not wrong. Girl, you hate it when I'm too high. But that's where I belong, where I belong..."

"If I overdose, bae, are you gon' drop with me? I don't even wanna think about that right now. Let's get too high; reach a new high. Take the shrooms and the pills at the same time..."

From his lyrics, it's evident that Juice WRLD was fully aware of the dangers of his drug use, but he was powerless to stop. He was addicted, and addiction is a disease. It takes over your life and controls you.

On the day of his death, Juice WRLD had taken several pills in an attempt to self-medicate his anxiety. He began having seizures and was later pronounced dead at the hospital. His cause of death was officially ruled as an accidental overdose of codeine and oxycodone.

Juice WRLD's addiction not only caused him great personal pain, but it also caused immense heartbreak for his fans and family. His fans were constantly worried about him, and his mother has spoken publicly about her son's battle with addiction. She has said that she hopes her son's death will be a lesson to others about the dangers of drug use.

It is tragic that Juice WRLD's life was cut short due to his addiction. However, his story can serve as a cautionary tale about the dangers of drug use. Hopefully, his story will help others to avoid the same fate. The dude lived a fast life and died young because of it. Y'all should learn from his mistakes! Don't do drugs, kids!

When you're blessed with success and talent as Juice WRLD had, it's a shame to see it all go to waste because of addiction.

I can't say all of that without saying this; I have never met Juice WRLD, but I would bet everything that I own that he did not want to get addicted to drugs. I believe that his use of drugs at a young age was by heavy influence from either peers or even family members. And let's keep it real, all the top rap artists nowadays rap about all the new drugs in their music. So, I'm sure he was looked at as the cool kid early on.

And that is the point. You may want to quit drinking or drug use, but the addiction will not let you. So, when you hear people say, "Just Say No." They are referring to the point in your life when you have full control over all the decisions in your life, and that is the moment when you are offered alcohol or drugs for the first time. "Just Say No!"

It's clear that this is easier said than done, but this same point in your life can be a personal road map to help you find your soberness, get you back on the right track, and save your life.

CHAPTER 11

THE NEW ERA OF DEADLY DRUGS: PILLS, LEAN, AND FENTANYL

Now, more than ever, drugs are becoming more and more popular. And with that popularity, comes danger. These days, it's not just about marijuana or meth anymore. Now, there are pills, lean, and fentanyl.

In the last few years, the new generation has turned to pills and lean (cough syrup) along with regular drinking. And of course, this new fentanyl craze is killing people. What's going on? Why are so many young people turning to drugs?

What are Pills, Lean, and Fentanyl and how do they differ from traditional drugs?

Pills, lean, and fentanyl are all new drugs that have become popular in the last few years. They are all highly addictive and can lead to death. Pills are typically taken orally while lean is drunk, and fentanyl is injected.

WHAT HAPPENS WHEN YOU TAKE PILLS?

Pills are extremely potent and can easily lead to an overdose. Pills can also cause organ damage, heart problems, and seizures. A single pill can contain a lethal dose of drugs, and come to think of it champs, why would you want to risk your life by taking something that could kill you?

WHAT HAPPENS WHEN YOU DRINK LEAN?

Drinking lean can lead to several different health problems. Lean is a highly concentrated form of cough syrup that contains a large amount of codeine. Codeine is an opioid pain medication that is extremely addictive and can lead to overdose and death. Codeine can also cause respiratory problems, heart problems, and seizures. Others include memory problems, listlessness, headache, blurred vision, dizziness, nausea, constipation, etc. I still can't wrap my head around why anyone would want to risk their life by drinking something that can kill them. But then again, I did the same shit back in my drinking days. Truthful any substance that alters your state of mind while being addictive, is a death wish.

WHAT HAPPENS WHEN YOU INJECT FENTANYL?

Fentanyl is a highly potent opioid pain medication that is extremely addictive and can also lead to overdose and death. Fentanyl can also cause respiratory problems, chest pain, discomfort, or difficulty, trouble breathing (irregular, fast or slow, or shallow breathing), lightheadedness, dizziness, etc. So again, why would anyone want to risk their life by taking something that can kill them?

You might be wondering why these new drugs are so popular. The answer is simple: they're cheap, easy to get, and very addictive. Pills, lean, and fentanyl are all highly addictive drugs that can be easily obtained by anyone, regardless of age.

What's even more alarming is that these drugs are becoming more and more available to young people. In fact, many young people are turning to these drugs because they're seen as a cheaper and more accessible alternative to traditional drugs like marijuana and cocaine.

Sadly, young dudes out there are dying because of these drugs. I mean, even if you don't die from taking them, the risk of becoming addicted is extremely high. So, man, just stay away from the shit altogether. They're not worth it.

As a young bright person, JUST SAY NO TO DRUGS! Your life is worth more than that! You may believe taking these drugs is a way to rebel against authority figures like parents and teachers, but all it's going to do is get you into trouble. I mean, straight up, rebelling has never helped anyone. It just gets you into more trouble than you were in before.

Again! I put it to you young dudes. Is taking these drugs really worth it? I mean just think about it, is getting high worth risking your life? Are these drugs really worth dying for? The moment you die, that's it. You're gone forever. Society needs the youth to help make this world a better place, not dead, destroyed, mentally and physically disturbed wrecks.

SECTION IV

SOLVING A PROBLEM

CHAPTER 12

D.U.I., 12 RECOVERY STEPS, AND A.A.

People who are alcohol-dependent are often resistant to counsel about quitting. What they are saying is, *"How did they find out? My drinking is tearing me apart, but I thought I was covering it well."* Admit to yourself that you are suffering from alcoholism. Be selfish and selfless at the same time. It is up to you to adjust yourself to be suitable for yourself and your family.

No Difference Between Supporter and Enabler.

Definition of an enabler: One that enables another to achieve an end: One who enables another to persist in self-destructive behavior (such as substance abuse) by providing excuses or by making it possible to avoid the consequences of such behavior.

From my experience, the enabler doesn't realize that they're causing you harm, but they are. This is a step that I took seriously. The first thing I noticed when I finally got 100% sober was that I didn't like being around people that had been drinking.

I Found My Soberness on September 1st, 2010.

At this time, my ex was still drinking every day. She was actually mad, and it seemed a little jealous when she realized that I had really stopped drinking. Maybe because I immediately stopped being her enabler by refusing not only to buy her any drinks but not even taking her to the store at all. We were similar when we got drunk. We both were loud, obnoxious, and known for saying stupid shit to people. Then we woke up the next day as if nothing had happened. So, it's safe to say that we were both enablers. But after September 1st, I was now the one being tormented by a drunk person's irrational thoughts. I couldn't stand to be around her anymore, so we parted ways. It would help if you got them out of your life as soon as possible. You can still love them and still like them, but you must love them from afar.

Be upfront with them and tell them the truth. "I have to distance myself from you because you hurt me more than you help me." It takes only one mistake to get your person in a failure state where they must start completely over from square one. Being fake to them will not make either of you happy if you are the one with the problem and cannot navigate the system for yourself.

Then, as I stated earlier, do what the counselors, judges, and advocates say. I'm sure this system works for some people, but in my case, I felt like it was setting me up for straight failure. You need a license to get a job. They want you to ride the bus and broke.

How can this not be the case when they take your license and charge you a crazy amount of fees that you can't pay because you can't get to your job? And the kind of job that I had required a driver's license. A dealership cannot insure you if your license is revoked. My time of being on probation was before Uber and Lift. I think these ride-share companies can help eliminate people drinking and driving, or at least, they should.

We didn't have this option; of course, we had the apparent opportunity not to drive drunk, but as I told the judge, "If I were sober, I would have never driven drunk." In other words, in my right mind, I wouldn't say I want to get drunk and then drive. If Uber was available, who knows? Maybe I would have taken another route. I am not playing the victim; as a matter of fact, for the first five years, I felt like I deserved punishment.

To this day, my wife doesn't drink because I don't. I believe I have messed up my opportunity to participate in the punishment. My five-year probation period ended in 2012, so I could have requested a hearing to get my license restored. But

I waited until the next year and attempted to do so numerous times every year after, and I've been turned down every year. I'll get to that later. But the point is that it is now 2022, and I'm sad that they still have not approved me to get my license back.

I've been sober for 12 years, but the state of Michigan did not believe me. I've had the magistrate or the person doing a hearing look me in my eyes and say, *"There is no way you're not still drinking; you're hiding something."*

I moved to Atlanta in 2014, and at some point, that became an issue. Again, I was told that he did not believe I lived in Georgia as opposed to Michigan. So, all these things, amongst others, were reasoning why I've been getting denied.

By this time, I felt like I paid my dues financially, emotionally, and spiritually. I could credit my rejections as systemic racism; what else could it be? Every magistrate that I appeared in front of made it seem like I personally owed them something. I felt the need to let this particular magistrate know

I didn't quit drinking because it cost me a lot of money or because the state of Michigan told me needed to.

I quit so I could reach my fullest potential in life, and I believe the systems are set up for failure; not having a license can deter you from achieving that potential. In 2018, I could not be silent any longer. I was approved for a restricted license that required me to pass a driving test and have a breathalyzer installed on my car for a year, and if I didn't get any strikes, I would be granted my full driver's license. After being denied year after year, the breathalyzer was my new norm.

Remember that this was ten years after my last offense and years of being sober. Still, I was excited about this small amount of freedom I was granted because one of the most important things I realized is that driving is a privilege. But with that privilege came a cost: $1400 to have it installed and a $300 every two months maintenance fee.

I felt very confident about this task because I was sober. After it was installed, I handed in these instructions.

HOW TO TAKE A TEST

1. *When you turn on the vehicle's ignition, the unit will activate, and the LCD will display WAIT ####. The device is preparing for a test. Take this time to drink WATER to eliminate breath contaminants.*

2. *Once the unit has initialized, the LCD will display the word BLOW.*

3. *You can only take a test when the LCD displays the word BLOW.*

4. *The best way to take a proper test is to blow steadily into the unit's mouthpiece for approximately 2 seconds and then transition to hum by saying "WHO." Keep blowing steadily during the transition. During the test, the LCD will display the word TEST.*

5. *Keep blowing into the mouthpiece while humming "WHO" until the unit clicks and the sound of the beep changes to a higher tone to let you know when to stop (approximately 7 seconds).*

6. *If you do not complete the test, the LCD will display the word ABORT, followed by the reason.*

7. *After completing the test, the LCD will display the word ANALYZING.*

8. *The unit will then analyze the breath sample and display PASS, WARN, FAIL, or VIOL.*

9. *During regular operation of the unit, the LCD will display "*," indicating engine running.*

AFTER YOU TAKE A TEST, 1 OF 4 THINGS WILL HAPPEN:

1. *The LCD will show the word PASS, and you may now start your vehicle.*

2. *The LCD will show the word WARN, and you may now start your vehicle.*

3. *The LCD will show the word FAIL, and you will not be able to start your vehicle.*

4. *The LCD will show the word VIOLATION, and you will not be able to start your vehicle.*

My first thought was that the success rate must be pretty low because the steps are extensive. The LCD display will show the word ABORT, and you will not be able to start your vehicle. Especially when you blow into the device, you have to loudly hum for about 30 seconds before it registers your alcohol levels.

This was even more humbling than my first time at an A.A. meeting when I had to stand up in front of strangers and admit I was an alcoholic. Not to mention that once your car is started, you are required to blow every 15 minutes during your drive. And if you miss or don't hear it, it counts as a violation.

Here Are the Other Non-alcohol Violations.

ABORT is generally caused by blowing too hard "ABORT HARD," for not a long enough period "ABORT EARLY," or not performing the voice tone properly "ABORT HUM." When you blow an ABORT or a FAIL, you must take and pass another breath test before your vehicle starts. After blowing a FAIL, the LCD will display FAIL, cycle back to WAIT for ##, and then BLOW.

An ABORT will require you to take another test. Once your vehicle is started, the device will ask for a random retest by beeping and indicating BLOW plus a timer reading. Failure to take these retests is a violation. The retest timer gives you 6 minutes to safely pull over and take the test if you are not comfortable testing while driving. If you fail to take the retest, the unit will indicate "MISSED TEST." This will result in a lost violation.

As I stated, I lived in Atlanta, so I also needed to apply for a hardship to monitor the breathalyzer in Georgia. After having the breathalyzer on the car for ten months, I got some dental work done. The medicated mouthwash caused a violation with the breathalyzer.

After humming into this device that looked like an old-school car phone from the 90s a few more times, the car started. On my next maintenance visit, I was told that I had a violation of my records. Two days later, my car was disabled. I had a video hearing informing the magistrate about my dental visit. He approved for the vehicle to be restarted, but he extended my time with the breathalyzer for two more months.

So, now, I was looking at 14 months instead of

12, which was fine for me. Right at the tail end of the initial 12 months, I received a letter from the breathalyzer company saying that they could no longer service my car in Georgia because my hardship had expired, and I needed to contact the state of Michigan.

After about a month of waiting, Michigan finally approved the hardship. Unfortunately, by this time, the state of Michigan had already violated me because my car had been sitting in my driveway, with no way to start it. The battery died which is a violation on its own, but even though Michigan knew I could not get the car serviced in Georgia, they still counted the missed appointments against me, and they revoked my license. I showed up to the video hearing like a proud student turning in makeup homework right before midterms. The magistrate ignored all my receipts and paperwork. *"If I need any of the items that you have, I'll let you know where to mail them,"* he stated.

In his next effort to be superior, my residence was again questioned. Why would I apply for a hardship if I did not live in Georgia? He ended the hearing by saying, *"Do you have anything else to add?"* Ten days later, I received a letter stating that my license was entirely revoked, and I had to provide proof that I was a Georgia resident. I had an appeal about 60 days later, and the same guy denied me.

It's hard for me to believe that the court system would assign the same magistrate that denied me the first time, to hear my appealed case. This time he was not listening to anything I had to say and denied me again with a 12-month waiting period to apply again and start all over.

Every person I've been around in the last eight years has never seen me drink. I am somewhat praised for being sober. I have been a sponsor to people with drinking issues, and I mentor the youth.

So, underlying all the penalties and fees that the system gives you, I learned about alcoholism and more significantly, knowing myself. And to be honest, I realized it on my own; with that, I can help other people, and that's what it's all about. When you get people, like me, who pay their debt to society, please give them the affirmation after that debt is paid. You can't make up a debt that must be paid but deny the restoration of their rights even after they pay the debt you set.

The system changes its goal halfway through to meet their needs to demean and break individuals. Install judges from among the reformed people who have experienced the reality of the disease of alcoholism. Stop allowing people with vendettas to sit in review and judgment.

A prayer, 12 Steps, and Alcoholics Anonymous were not my recovery process. They were opportunities for reflection. I questioned what it would take for me to get back to the place I was before drinking and alcoholism. I wanted to get back to ME. I tried to get back to being an example. I began to break it down into years. I would calculate that I had not drunk for 20 years. I only drank for ten years. I was still winning. I thought about the fact that I had never been to jail or been in any beef sober. I was giving it all that I had to get to that sober place, but I was not physically ready. I quit every Monday morning in 2004 and went back to it every Monday night.

Years later, by the time that I had 3 D.U.I.s, I would quit drinking for short periods at a time but somehow ended up drinking again. By this time, the courts had handed down their suggested methods of help. The first thing they teach you is how to drink; they tell you precisely when the alcohol wears off. I don't know if they do this on purpose, but once I learned this, I would still drink. But I would stop drinking around 8:00 p.m. so that it was out of my system by the morning.

I wanted to defy the system. I knew how to get over on the system. But I was risking a lot, like I said it's an automatic year in prison for a fourth D.U.I. charge. With this thought in my mind, I finally grew up and stopped risking my life in 2010. Remember, my mission to stop drinking started in 2004, driven by a popular song. The song talked about stories of people struggling to get out of terrible situations. It resonated because I wanted something different. The songwriter wrote the song based on real troubles people have. I wanted to be a specimen—an example of or model of success, upward mobility, and recovery.

Every time I heard the song, I wanted to cry and

change my life. The singer was my favorite artist at the time. When he came out with the music on a gospel album, he showed the other side. There were others out there that were looking to change their lives. I played it on repeat. I did not listen to anything else, still drinking with tears in my eyes and telling myself that I was tripping and that I knew that I would quit one day. It took 6 years, but it happened. I still listen to this song today from the other side of the bottle.

I was not worried about my health; I was worried about my reputation. I would wake up and call all the people I was with the night before and ask. "Hey, I'm just calling to see if I did any stupid shit last night." I wished it would be a commendable experience, but it was excruciating. My fears were confirmed each morning.

My home was robbed. My reputation was so bad that people said that I deserved it. I thought to myself, "Is this what people are thinking about me now?" Yet, everyone around me was a drinker as well. We all influenced each other. I will say that I was an alcoholic. But there are levels. I was not at the top of the list. I could function at a high level.

Other than that, I'm no different from my peers, even when quitting drinking. It might be hard to believe that as drunk and unbearable as I was, I was conscious and observant, not only of myself but of human behavior in general. For example, I noticed that everyone who plans to stop drinking plans to stop on a Monday or the first of the month. This includes me. I stated earlier that I found my soberness on September 1st, 2010.

Recovery Inspired

There are always two sides to every story. I took something good from Alcoholics Anonymous. I took the 12 Steps, especially how you speak honestly to yourself. You must identify that you have a problem. That 12-step process is dead on. Yet, it would help if you had something to remember it with.

You must identify what life means to you. If what matters to you is going to work and coming home, that is different from wanting to take over the world. I have never seen a sloppy drunk person take over the world. The following method and comparison were applied two weeks before I quit.

My view of the situation had to be clear based on my standards so that my choices could be different.

Changing your goal and intention is the only way to make sustainable progress when you are impaired. I was not going to fail in recognizing my potential. A change was necessary because of my goals, and I knew the ME was possible.

Me in This Moment.

The other wake-up call for me was the comparison between me and others. Luckily and unluckily, I saw young people hooked on crack during the crack epidemic. I remember how we used to talk wrong about crackheads. We were kids, and we always thought crackheads were old, but I realized later in life as an adult that they were only in their 20s.

Remember, the crack epidemic was so new that we didn't know it was new. It was not just how my friends talked about people who abuse crack cocaine. It was how society looked at them in movies and other media. They were not looked at as people who had worth. They were not treated as contributors to the world. Seeing that some viewed or could view me as that lowly, disrespected person contradicted my view of myself.

The Goal You Choose.

It takes time to realize that you are a drinker. We would play basketball and have a cooler of 40s to drink afterward. That was just how we were. It was not a problem until the basketball, the social interaction, and the cool factor was gone. All that was left was the 40s. They became the focus, the goal, and the reward for nothing in particular.

The Company You Keep.

Recovery stifled what I don't like about the programs offered or in most cases, ordered to help you quit is that we are systematically brainwashed to stand up to specific standards. People will use your weakness to keep you where they want you. I look back and not only consider myself as a social crackhead but also all the people I was around. They couldn't help me improve because I didn't want to, and vice versa.

For example, I have not learned the words of the

12-steps prayer. When you go before any board, they ask you to recite the prayer. If you don't get it right, you are denied. The outcome desired is not breaking the will or conformity to an ideal in the general sense. The result expected is to stop drinking. I believe that a strong will and the ability to make your own decisions are critical to a sustainable life change.

Being told that I must do this or that flies in the face of autonomy and personal responsibility. I was an automaton to alcohol long enough to understand the difference between my decisions and pressure, obligation, or addiction pulling my strings. I refuse to replace one disease for another. I choose to be free from outside influences and responsible for myself.

Learning that prayer is where I draw a line in the sand. I told a magistrate that the system is rigged to diminish the former drinker, crush the spirit, and conform to them. They are attempting to fit in some way to a standard, example, or predisposition that offers them no solace but to do what they are told. That is why many drink in the first place.

I told him, "You set up these rules and programs with these procedures and actions to keep people down. It would help if you believed in these programs because you put people through them. But you can't believe they work because I was denied five times." I was communicating that my outcome was a cessation of drinking but also autonomy, self-respect, and a clearer vision for my life. Yet, without their stamp of approval, my enlightenment was rendered dim. I didn't quit because of the system. I quit because I wanted to.

One of the magistrates on a panel denied my application for license reinstatement because he said, *"I don't believe that you have stopped drinking."* He did not understand how alcoholics work to silence the pattern of alcoholism. He had no clue about the markers of the functioning alcoholic versus the indicators of genuine autonomy and recovery from substance abuse.

CHAPTER 13

SETUP FOR FAILURE

I have been denied multiple times for different issues that felt, to me, like racism. I have never been in front of a board of my peers—people who looked like me. And fundamentally, the system is constructed to fail those that enter it. The designation of alcoholic dooms you to a lifetime of being second-guessed and judged at the mercy of other people's so-called wisdom.

Thankfully, they only hold power over the driver's license. They cannot hold me back from my professional pursuits, no matter how it seems they would like to. The year 2008 was the last D.U.I.

I have it on my record. I have gone through the required protocols and still have not received a driver's license.

Setup for Failure

The system is not set up for you or me to win. When you don't have an alcoholism issue, an alcoholic is your best reason not to take a drink. After you get into the system, you are always in it. I have not drunk in 12 years; great, but I must still go in front of people who are allowed to judge me even though they don't know me.

My emotions run high when discussing this because it is yet another area where people can exercise the insidiousness of racism, ableism, and prejudices. I don't care if a person does not like a person because of the color of their skin. I don't care if a person thinks they are better than me. I don't care what your misconceptions are before viewing the evidence. My issue is that a person feels they can judge another person while denying the evidence.

That is fundamentally unfair. You don't get to

rule based on your gut feelings about the case. You don't get to cite your experiences from the past without a view of the evidence in front of you. Whoever gave the same people the power to create the law and the penalty is insane.

The person who makes the penalty should be a person who is in recovery. If not, all you are doing is creating a box for people. In marketing, we know that 1% of people will buy no matter what the marketing is or who it is from.

This is a law in marketing. One percent, at least, of people will drink in excess. Many of them are going to get caught. Law firms will tell you that 1 in every 220 adults has a D.U.I.

CBS News reported in 2015 that close to 2% of American adults admit to driving while intoxicated. People are falling prey to alcoholism. But that does not stop the machine from moving. That is the machine. For example, when you go to a bar, they tell you that drinking and driving is illegal. Yet, bartenders are serving people that they know must get home. The State sells liquor licenses to bars that sell as many drinks as they can drink in one night. They are sent off to drive home endangering the lives of everybody on the road.

People who need help don't get any attention from the system other than going to jail. Rehab centers, lawyers, and municipalities are financially enhanced when people violate the laws expressing their alcoholism disease. What incentive do these institutions have to stop the alcohol trade or help those with the condition to heal? I am only hoping that the system works.

If you put me through all the classes and actions to gather signatures and character references and to test to support my case for sobriety, you cannot then turn around and tell me what you don't believe. Your belief is not my issue. The work I put in is the evidence to be evaluated. In sobriety, I am not only overcoming the disease. I am overcoming the stigma, the shame, the restitution, the guilt, and the loss I have endured.

A person in recovery often has the task of rebuilding their life from nothing, having lost everything.

For a person to sit in judgment based on their feelings is disrespectful at most, minor and criminal at worst.

People Who Second-Guess You

It is difficult to share my experiences AND instruct people on how to think. My way of thinking preceded my desire to quit. I am definitely in a select 5% of those in recovery. My addictive behavior was a pattern bolstered by the environment, peer influences, and possibly genetics. It was never how I saw myself. My recovery centered around returning to that vision of myself as whole, capable, and better without the alcohol.

The first time I went to the clinic, I was court-ordered. I had to sit in rooms with people I felt were not as accomplished as me. I began to feel like I was answering my probation officers. But my recovery was not about answering others. It was about answering myself.

Most people with a problem must take the system-derived method of quitting. I went, and

I was buzzing. I was only there because I was forced to. I knew I was buzzing. I was not paying attention to anyone. I got up and started talking. I began to stand on my soapbox concerning the system. I felt so passionate about the setup that is the system built around liquor production, sales, consumption, punishment, and recovery. I was a contradiction. I knew I was. But no one else knew it.

That Is How Sober AF Was Born.

When you stand and say something with authority, people must listen. Knowing that a year in jail will not help if drinking is a disease. My response to the guy that said that he did not believe I quit drinking was defiant. "At some point, you created a business out of the alcoholism in this country… so stop fucking with me and give my license back."

I knew he was not qualified to make the determination he was making. I would rather he knew how to move with someone with a disease. He did not realize the impact of denying me a license. He did not know how dire that denial was. He had never been in that situation. Systemic racism is the problem. He does not have to be racist to stand behind a racist system.

When people do not have the experience of being in trouble or without, they cannot judge those who have been in a position of lack. Racism is skin deep. Prejudice is judging without all the information. Bigotry is a matter of thinking you are better than another person. You can deny me by a piece of paper or convictions. But you are not better than me. In life, you don't have what I have. This man would not see anyone who is a drinker as on his level. He chose to attempt to keep me low.

He had the authority to keep me under the provision of the system. It was as simple as keeping a breathalyzer on the car. He was happy to stay even with that chain on me. When someone has power over you, empowered by systemic racism, and he asks, *"Do you have anything to add before we wrap up?"* Every time I heard that phrase, it was a negative result.

Battling the System From the Wrong Side of the Desk

In my first D.U.I., I accepted the system as the rule of law. Subconsciously, I assumed that they had authority. There was a time when I felt like I deserved the penalty. My 16-year-old employee would drive me to my probation appointments. I allowed the roles to be reversed. I could not discipline him at work and feel comfortable being driven by him to appointments.

On the second, I had to turn in my license plate. I realized then that it was not my plate. My mind was already working. On the third, they make you take all the cars you own out of your name. They know you will likely sell the vehicle to a family member. You are barred from doing that. If you attempt to sell to a family member, your license is revoked. If you are trapped in a situation, you only have to say what you want to hear. It would help if you did what they wanted you to do. You must embrace the role of the bad guy. If you do not, you will have a hard road.

They want to hear you say that you are an alcoholic.

They want you to be beneath them. They make you say your name and say, "I am an alcoholic." On the third D.U.I., I had something inside of me that said I could do whatever I wanted. As a career, I shoot real movies with real actors in Hollywood. That creative power does not stop with making movies.

My life is a movie that I script with my actions. I make the rules. This is my world. I was created powerful by God. Their practices are done with the expectation that I will break them. I had to work the system in my favor if I had any chance at sobriety. I had to live up to the person that I know myself to be.

Remember that people look at the alcohol company as a person. We drinkers are the foolish ones putting money in these individuals' pockets. But the lesson for me was the legal status of corporations. I sold the vehicles to my company. I still own them.

The registrations are also in the name of the company. The beauty is that the company has legal status. The rule was that you could not have a car in your name. I have had at least 30 vehicles without a license. If you talked to the celebrities I know, they would not be able to tell you about my past. No one would ever know.

CHAPTER 14

WHY I QUIT

We must individualize ourselves and the effects. The slogan is "Drunken words are sober thoughts." You have a built-in Americanized filter when you are sober. You lose that filter when you are drunk. You know you cannot run up to someone and say what you want. We have Cancel Culture and Apology.

Cancel Culture is a regular cycle of life today. Alcohol is liquid courage. Someone always wants to fight. We perceive popularity as toughness and toughness as popular. That is a trope in all our movies. You have been trained to be that. You may not be that tough in real life, but you drink and get the courage to be that person. You lose your filter and live within that fantasy of popularity and toughness.

I remember after I was fingerprinted and booked for my 3rd D.U.I. I saw a young guy standing for his 4th D.U.I. He was only 21, and to hide his fear, he was playing tough. The total environment was crazy. The dude in the cell next to me hung himself because he molested a 5-year-old girl. He knew that the general population would kill him. I questioned why they would put me in that situation. I also asked why I would put myself in that situation. I am a master at projecting myself into different positions. I saw a 21-year-old who acted as I acted at that age. He was cocky. His cockiness reminded me of when I borrowed my friend's car with the burglary kit in the trunk. I saw myself in him, remembering how I went back to the club bragging.

In the back of my head, I was sure I was not supposed to be there. I saw how far my goals and aspirations were from where I found myself. I had matured and experienced life well beyond this 21-year-old's level. I had built a quarter-million-dollar house and done tremendous things. I felt for him, but I also felt bad for myself. I saw myself in him.

The following day, his cockiness faded instantly as he realized that he was going to Jackson Penitentiary for a year. He was on his 4th D.U.I. I could see the anguish and remorse I would have.

No different when I was let go because the officer's radio alerted him of a more important 187 in the area. When I was pulling away, I did not have thoughts about relief. I had been driving intoxicated so long that this was normal. I did not want to get in trouble, but driving drunk was a lifestyle.

My mindset was about getting away with something. Intoxicated people are not concerned about laws and social acceptance. Now, I desire to be an advocate for people who have a drinking problem. I believe that alcoholism is a weapon of the system. I tell people not to drink. I write about the mindset of change and growth required to overcome the disease.

The message is not limited only to alcoholism and recovery. The lessons of autonomy, self-determination, justice, and progress find application in all areas of life. The challenge we all have is a view of the world as material, infinite, and disposable. Energy is not created or destroyed, only recycled.

All the talk that we do about possession is frivolous. All this is ours. We are all here to take care of the earth. Get people to start thinking that way, and there is no way they will fall victim to the system. Few things that we worry about are worth the energy.

My fourth book, "Poor Dad Only" talks about the system all the way through. Do not insult my intelligence with stupid shit. If I only have a poor dad, I still have a foundation from which to make healthy decisions and progress. Stop being dismissive of the struggle that people go through in their lives.

Contribute to their sense of something greater within themselves rather than holding them down under the guise of upholding the law, a rule, or a standard. What good is a standard that diminishes a person's humanity?

Every day, we protest injustice. Every day, those protests are turned into something different. I watched the news displaying mothers with the same anguish and no way out. No matter how many times they get in front of the microphone and cry, they are not satisfied.

Many people receive a pat on the back for supporting the system. Too many profits from investing in the system that maintains the status quo of injustice. All I can do is write this book. All I can do is bring attention to the injustice of creating the vice, the temptation, the lifestyle, the mistakes, the penalty, the legal repercussions, the barriers to restitution, and the determining factors of my limitation. BUT what they don't know is that I am Mann Robinson. I realize that all these are constructs. All these are made up. I can still operate to my fullest in the context of this faulty, rigged world. I can still rise in the morning, raise my children, run businesses, shoot movies, and make way for my children and others who may decide to exit an oppressive system.

My Kids

Children need discipline, structure, and an environment that supports the development of appropriate filters. Filters are important. The elimination of filters is a problem for the development of fertile minds. I used to tell my kids that I was drinking Kool-Aid. "Grab me my Kool-Aid." I would lie to them because my train of thought was not altogether healthy.

My son was 9 when I took him with me to my cousin's house. I was drunk as fuck and trying to hype my son up to race against his cousin. I was all in his face. He had no choice. "I will give you $1000 if you race against him." He finally gave in and was smoked by my cousin's son. He was embarrassed not by losing but by his drunk father.

I had lost my sense of self. I see myself in the top

20% of people. When I am acting like 80%, it eats away at me. The 80/20 proposition is vital to me. I was driving in the car with my daughter. I was not supposed to be driving. "There goes the PoPo."

She prepared to do whatever it took to conceal that I was driving. I recognized in her voice that she was beginning to mistrust the police. This is what I was teaching. This is what my children were enduring and observing. Years later, when they found out, we had a long talk about my admission and my apology. I didn't sugarcoat the past or the current situation. I was working to restore the appropriate filter in their minds. I had lost time, but I took the opportunity.

I remember my son calling to check in one night. He called me from a party and told me he was not drinking. *"Dad. I want you to know that what you taught us is working."* No drink that I had ever made me feel as good as that. Genetics are strong. They are what they are. Just because my kids are mine doesn't mean they will follow me in everything.

My daughter is an entrepreneur to her core. She

ran my computer store in Detroit for a time at a super young age. I have always been proud of the adults they have grown into. My son is the same. He wants to be an entrepreneur, not working for anyone but himself. He has the mindset to invest in the stock market. He wants to invest in multi-family properties. This is due to the shift in my attitude and activity. It was also a conversation and non-conversations.

In movies, the action and the dialogue eat up the real estate of the script. You can learn as much from the action as the dialogue. When I switched and made my conversation match my efforts, the impact on the audience was more significant. The audience is my children. It takes a village to raise a child. You are around people that influence you all day.

Drinking is the number one celebration in events from the Super Bowl to music videos. The influence is strong from family and media. If your kids pick up what you are drinking, they may consume it as well. They ask you in programs if your parents were drinkers. You don't have to drink just because your parents drink. You can still choose not to. But the choice is still yours.

Drinking alters your reflexes and your decision-making. Both these are about self-protection. Even if you make it past D.U.I., traffic accidents, and vehicular homicide, your children may adopt alcoholism and find karma in their lives.

The Holistic Approach Identifies that drinking is a disease

After drinking for so long, you need help. They tell you to say your name. The alcoholic is me. Just imagine if you take all the stress out of this world. You make money, live life, and love your kids. That is what drinking does for you.

If you are sad, drinking clears your mind. If you need to wind down, alcohol will smooth your nerves. If you can take the time to imagine, you will see that every problem we have is artificial. Bills, courts, and more are artificial. Anything our creator made is free from stress. Love, compassion, nature, and more are not stressful.

When you hide the disease, you don't get the opportunity to be looked at to receive help. The denial makes you an alcoholic as much as the behavior does. To see the disease for what it is, you must visit the social, physical, and spiritual effects on your life.

Social

Alcoholism affects you as well as your family and friends. It also impacts the people you reach with your vision, talents, and sober actions. Everything I did, impacted my children. It took away time and money. It caused me to miss events.

Alcoholism is your disease. But it infects the lives of all those around you. Refuse to pass the infection on to them. Refuse to replace those positive social progress opportunities with the frivolous lifestyle and interactions of other alcoholics.

CHAPTER 15

HOW I GOT TO QUIT ALCOHOLISM

When you go for a gun license, they ask if you drink. The reason for that is that most people can talk out their problems. Humans can face adversity and challenge with grace. But with alcohol, they know that people will act in ways they would not if sober. If you have a gun, the outcome of a simple argument could be devastating.

Drinking is not a sustainable choice. It can only limit your potential. Quitting on your own allows you to take control of your life in a new way—with new tools. You can be a specimen—an example of a person who steps out of the rigged system to create opportunities for something more than what is artificial. Wealth, policy, status, and fame are constructs that are inferior to us.

The Steps

Generally, it would help if you individualized yourself. You cannot compare yourself to anyone else. Don't compare yourself to people who are doing well while drinking or are perceived to be. Everyone wants to emulate the top 3% of people. The challenge is that we are not all at that level statistically.

Those that are among the least of us are often beset with addiction or distractions. No one is more important than another. Take a step back and realize that the measurement of the percentages is artificial. That percentage you aspire toward is no longer a reality no matter how you tell yourself that you are worthy of better. Drinking boxes you into a maintenance reality versus an expanded reality.

Don't fault yourself for attempting to quit and failing. Keep going. With each attempt, you learn more about what you need to do. Realize that you are a living self-help book, rather than taking another man's success as an example. Start flipping the pages of your self-help book and reviewing what you learn. It is a tricky discussion.

Drinking and being under its influence seems to be an enhancement to creativity. It does not make you more creative. It removes your filter. You can accomplish the same thing through practice and mindfulness. The danger is that you may think that you need the substance to be creative.

The substance gets into your body, and you crave it physically. This is the physical connection to the mind in a vicious cycle. We are all owners of this planet. In the percentage that you are born, you build. Consider the lion and his position at the top of the savannah percentage. He has no money or any other man-made items but is still king.

The metrics we are using are unimportant and lacking value. We should always revert to our purpose for being. We were put here to take care of the planet. I am not saying that we live in the jungle and live off the plants and take care of the earth. If you get stuck on all the artificial things, you falter.

If your mind lives in the jungle without the trappings of artificial things or if we focus on taking care of the earth as intended, we approach life differently. We are not unsettled like we were before. You see purpose and create a vision differently. The foolery is less of a distraction. We move toward our aim, and our objective is enough.

The Brainwashing

We are not born to play basketball or be a singer. How could we be born to do anything man-made? The only thing we were born to do is learn and progress. Learning creates progression. Progression creates a desire to continue forward. Drinking alters all of that. Our bodies are programmed to be brainwashed (led to understanding).

The body has that exact mechanism to be

brainwashed. The body can be trained to the point where it craves alcohol. This spurs addiction. Addiction is a disease. Progress is the core intention. You continue to progress, but you create a pull in a different direction with alcohol. Alcohol supports the person and experience that you desire. It becomes more encompassing as you lose perspective; the other part is that you get the benefits temporarily from the drinking experience.

Temporary because you have a hangover, a fender bender, loss of family ties, and experiences that impact your life and happiness. If you know that brainwashing is not a bad word, you know that choice is what makes things happen. Unfortunately, drinking is not one of those things you can choose mentally and be done with it. Alcoholism has a physical component as well. Brainwashing is often a product of fear.

My mom used to say, *"You listen to rap, so I am going to rap for you. Hell and jail. Hell and jail. Don't do that because of Hell and jail."* We make decisions out of fear. The alternative is to make your choices based on careful reasoning.

Drinking eliminates the ability to project themselves through the risk and into the later reward or punishment. You need the information to make the best decisions. That is where you realize that brainwashing is not wrong. The rewards come through seeking and informing our choices. That is why I know my reward is this world. If you know what it's all made up, you can project. Personally, the cool thing is to quit drinking.

When I began with that process, I retrained the popularity toward another indicator. There was no difference between the Every-Monday Resolution and the decision to quit. There was serious business going on in my head.

I was dead serious each time. I looked at peer pressure as a sign of weakness for me. I now look at it as a weakness by them. I needed to put my mind and body in the same place.

The people were not going to put me in that place. I got drunk as fuck. If I put myself in a position of non-recovery, it would work. My mind was already ready. I had to get my body there. The brainwashing worked, and the most powerful feeling was that I was better than everyone else. I was better than anybody breathing. Yet, the way I was living was not what I was doing. I had to wake up in the morning and apologize to everyone before I could know what I had done. I reviewed my family. My sister never drank. For my brother, the only time he drank was at my behest, and he got in trouble.

My father drank but slowed down. I reviewed my mother's immediate family. All of them were drinkers, but only two were at my level. I didn't like their lives. I checked my father's family, and it was only one uncle, and he was the crackhead of the family. I felt that I was the crackhead of my family. I asked what made me go back to drinking. I was only ready mentally.

Physically, I was not ready. My body craved it. When I get super drunk, it takes three days. Knowing that I knew this would happen, and the fact that I have been actually seen as a crackhead was all I need, so on August 31, 2010, I decided to go to the store and buy a 24-pack of Budweiser for the last day of drinking. I drank the whole 24-pack. I woke up in the morning feeling like someone had shot me. I was sick as fuck, but I was happy to be sick. I never craved it after that, and that was officially my very last day of drinking. Now, I could tell myself who I was. I could accomplish much more.

CHAPTER 16

STAY SOBER AS FUCK

What is staying sober as fuck like? It is a lifestyle; I mean, being sober is a lifestyle. It should be our original lifestyle, everybody's original lifestyle. Nobody is born drunk.

In some cases, maybe your parents (your mama was drunk when she had you), but still, nobody is born with a drunken lifestyle. So, my original lifestyle is to be sober as fuck, and that's what my mind is and will remain.

To find soberness again is to realize where my mind is when I am sober, allowing me to stay sober. I do not consider drinking as incredible as I used to when I was in my 20s, or even in my 30s. I could assume we have always been told that drinking was only meant for grown people when it should be taught that it could become an addiction.

Yes, they tell you that you have to be grown to drink, but once you become grown and go through all these problems, you almost lose everything; you almost kill people, even nearly kill yourself. Now, looking at other people doing the same thing, you realize that it is meant not just for grown people but for immature people. It is for kids; it is for very naive people.

That's not me; I'm not living that lifestyle anymore. My lifestyle is one of a specimen, one I would want everybody to be like. I want to be everything that people think they cannot be. I want to be that, and I am that. That way, when you leave this earth, you do not just leave a legacy of material things, but something you create, and your family can consider a more legitimate and sustainable gift.

To me, legacy is more than what you can show

other people and what lives you have changed. This is because people change lives daily. Everyone changes life negatively or positively. Consider a situation of somebody who robs the bank, scaring a woman at the reception or the teller behind the money-counting machine to the point that she is too scared to be a teller again. This automatically means he just negatively changed her life.

So, everybody can change somebody's life; one person can change other people's lives every day. If anyone's life would change positively, I want it to be that I will be the one to be remembered for the impact.

When they say, "I remember that from him, how he changed my life for the better. I also want to change my life to follow his, and I want to do the same as he is." I want that when they speak of me.

My mother died in 2005. I stated this before, but she has never seen the side of me as a grown person. The side of me she has always seen is getting in trouble or acting stupid. One time, she had to take a gun for me because she saw me several times arguing with my girlfriend and getting into arguments with customers. She's seen obviously everything. When she passed away, I was still a drunk. She never got a chance to see her son sober as fuck, and I'm sure she would have been proud of that.

The hardest part of being such a mess as my mother's last memories of me was that she was impacted by drunk driving back when I was in high school. One day, she was driving home from the store in our brand-new car that my father had just bought to win her back. And she was hit by a drunk driver. Luckily, she wasn't hurt badly, but she was forced to have to deal with something just as bad. The driver was over the top drunk and a full-blooded racist, forcefully approaching my mother while constantly calling her a stupid nigger! She was alone and scared. My father got the call and darted to the crash site. The driver continued, but he was in more danger than he realized.

At that point, my father was the real problem, but he held his composure due to the police presence, which was the best move because the driver had multiple D.U.I.s and was sent to prison later that year.

Watching my mother go through, not only the accident but also the trial puts a different meaning to "Mothers Against Drunk Driving."

But somehow, I seemed to forget all of this and become one of the things that she hated the most. A fucking drunk!

When I discovered that this was the case and I started putting forth efforts to quit, I didn't attempt to quit alcohol altogether. I focused on giving up what I drank the most, which was beer. But I noticed when I quit drinking beer periodically, I would automatically go to another vice. And that vice was something sweet: carbs, chocolate, ice cream, or whole jars of peanut butter.

Eventually, it got to a point where these things started making me throw up. For example, I would eat two doughnuts, stand up, start feeling queasy and weird, walk to the back of my house or wherever I was, put my head in the sky, and boom; my body would reject everything I just ate.

I would start talking to myself about it, "So, what the heck are you doing Mann?" But of course, my mind was not ready to quit drinking, so I got back into drinking again. But my body was rejecting everything that I consumed, and this went on for years.

Until September 1, 2018, after drinking all night, I told myself I was never gonna drink again. I didn't have an urge to replace the vice anymore. I didn't want sugar. I didn't want shit. I just wanted it to be sober.

So, I took on health; that's what I wanted, to be sober as fuck and be the healthiest. Then, there were a bunch of diets out there, but the **Keto Diet** made the most sense to me. Because everything in the keto diet that you canned had been making me vomit in the first place. Sugar, carbs, alcohol, and beer after one sip made me throw up.

When I read up on the keto diet, they called it the Atkins diet, back then. The Atkins diet I considered fun because I was able to eat eggs, bacon, and cheese pretty much to eat all day—breakfast food all day. It was fun. No alcohol; drink a lot of water.

I thought to myself that it worked and made a lot of sense. "I'm only cutting out the things that my body doesn't want anyway. This is gonna be a cakewalk." And it was.

I started adding other things like vegan into it. I stayed away from bread and sugar and all that, as I said, and started working out seven days a week. The entire fat beer belly was gone. I had a six-pack.

People in my neighborhood couldn't believe it. My boy said, "What? Are you a model?" I'm like, "Yeah, Nigga. I'm a model. I'm a director. I'm a writer. I'm a producer. I'm a rapper. I'm a business owner. I'm an entrepreneur, but I'm not a drunk. I'm sober as fuck!"

I want to encourage everybody else to stay sober. So, if you enjoyed the book, thank you for reading, and live the rest of your life and journey sober and healthy as fuck.

Thank you!

CONCLUSION

So, I think the main takeaway is to understand your limits and potential; do you know what I mean? I mean, with all that being said, some things in life are simply out of reach, and there are also some things we can do to change that.

Therefore, people might say many different things to you, like "You'll never quit drinking," "You can never be a model," or "Maybe it doesn't work for you." But the important thing to know is your limits, and I think for me, if I'm just not ready to quit drinking, then that was fine. But the point was to do it on my terms. So, I did it on my terms.

Now, more than ever, it's important to think about what it is you want to do with your life, and I think that's something we could all be doing more. Now, of course, don't overlook the fact that there might be some solutions out there for you, but at the end of the day, it really just comes down to self-knowledge and self-confidence.

I hope this was helpful for you guys! Thank you very much for reading the book. It's been a pleasure working on it, and I hope it was helpful to you as much as it was to me. Let's continue to be **SOBER AS FUCK!**

Made in the USA
Columbia, SC
12 November 2023